DATE DUE FOR RETURN

NEW ACCESSIONS

Spiegel

SPIEGEL

The Man Behind the Pictures

Andrew Sinclair

WEIDENFELD AND NICOLSON

LONDON

First published in Great Britain by
George Weidenfeld & Nicolson Limited,
91 Clapham High Street, London SW4 7TA
1987

ISBN 297 79210 5

Printed and bound in Great Britain by
Butler & Tanner Ltd, Frome and London

TO SONIA

Too much success is the only tragedy.
SPIEGEL

Contents

Illustrations

Trailer

"*If there were any recipe for being a producer,*" *Sam Spiegel said,* "*people would go to cooking school to get it. There are no rules. It's really a negative that makes you a success. You should never make a picture you are not excited about. You must feel that unless you make this picture you won't be able to sleep.*"

"*These are the accidents of history that prevent you from becoming a lampshade,*" *Spiegel said after fleeing from Nazi Germany when he was warned by his S.S. barber that they were coming for him that night.*

"*Ladies and gentlemen, please continue to be my guests. I am temporarily the guest of His Majesty's Government,*" *Spiegel said as he was led away from a party he was giving in the Dorchester Hotel in London. He was on his way to his trial at the Old Bailey.*

"*It's the old story, if you woke up in a motel with a dead whore who'd been stabbed, who would you call? D'you know, Sam Spiegel,*" *Billy Wilder said to John Huston in the years when the Hollywood saying was,* "*Spiegel can do anything except make a picture,*" *and the word to be* "*spiegeled*" *meant to be soothed, cajoled or conned.*

His act left Billy Wilder S.P. Eechless, but his friends did not change their names to Darryl Z.A. Nuck or Ernst L.U. Bitsch. "*If anyone knew how to ride out a loser,*" *Budd Schulberg wrote,* "*it was S.P. Eagle.*"

"*I was struck by a burst of patriotism,*" *Spiegel said on changing his name to S.P. Eagle.* "*My German name seemed particularly profane in the circumstances, so I renounced it.*"

I

"*Spiegel is the Thief of Baghdad,*" *Mary Anita Loos said,* "*but right out in the open. But socially and in a friendly way, everybody in Hollywood loved him.*"

"*A story of two old people going up and down a river,*" *Alexander Korda said of Spiegel's film* African Queen *with Humphrey Bogart and Katharine Hepburn.* "*You will be bankrupt.*"

"*Professional is one thing, politics is another,*" *Spiegel said to Marlon Brando in the stage delicatessen on Seventh Avenue.* "*Separate them.*" *Brando did and agreed to be directed by Elia Kazan in* On the Waterfront.

"*There is no story in Kwai without a bridge,*" *Spiegel said,* "*and the bridge acquires meaning only when it is destroyed. So you build the bridge to illustrate your point. The question of quarter of a million dollars is only a number on your cost sheet.*"

"*Hollywood without Spiegel is like Tahiti without Gauguin,*" *Billy Wilder said when Spiegel left for Europe to make his films such as* Suddenly Last Summer. *At the end of filming that, Katharine Hepburn spat in Spiegel's eye.* "*It's rather a rude gesture,*" *she said,* "*but at least it's clear what you mean.*"

"*He got class across without irritating you,*" *the film distributor Max Youngstein said about life on Spiegel's luxury yacht, the* Malahne, *while Joe Mankiewicz said after visiting Spiegel's penthouse on Park Avenue,* "*Sam Spiegel is the only Jewish cardinal in New York.*"

"*I have never forgiven him for getting me out of prison,*" *Robert Bolt said after writing the screenplay for* Lawrence of Arabia, *an expensive film that Spiegel defended by saying that he never used a thousand camels when only a couple of hundred would do. He won his third Oscar as a producer for the film.*

"*Sam Spiegel was one of the most cultured and enlightened people one could ever happen to meet,*" *wrote Edward Heath, once Prime Minister. Yet after the failure of his epic,* Nicholas and Alexandra, *Spiegel declared,* "*Do you expect a leopard to change his stripes? Truthfully, I would rather make a bad picture and make it my way than make a good picture and make it your way."*

When he was told that his last picture, Harold Pinter's Betrayal, *was a little picture, Spiegel said, "Is it, really? Do you worry in a painting about the size of the canvas?" Pinter himself said of Spiegel's major films. "When I say that he* made *all these films, I mean what I say. Total responsibility. Total dedication."*

Before his death on New Year's Eve, 1985, Spiegel said, "I believe in mortality, but not in inflicting it on myself."

"Sam Spiegel was the last of the giants," said Arthur Schlesinger at his memorial service. "His death was the end of a great chapter in the history of the cinema." Fred Zinnemann concurred. "If a producer is really creative, if he generates a project, it is important for him to run the show. But you can count people like that on the fingers of two hands. Korda, Thalberg, Selznick, Goldwyn, Zanuck, Spiegel. The other 'creative producers' are ridiculous. It is vanity."

CHAPTER ONE

Moving Pictures

*The existence of the Jews in the non-Jewish world is ... a sort of ghost
nation stalking the arena of world history.*

CHAIM WEIZMANN

Pictures of America were still and silent: drawings, etchings, lithographs,
daguerrotypes. They reached Middle Europe in the nineteenth century by
wooden ships and horse-drawn coaches, then by steamships and railroads.
At first, the pictures showed wildernesses and frontiers, herds of buffalo
and backwoodsmen, Indians and cowboys, scenes of Civil War or natural
disasters. Then the images of the United States began to change. Great
ports and cities appeared, capitols and churches, markets and bridges, and
by 1886, the image of freedom itself, the Statue of Liberty raising her torch
to those who sought to pass through the golden door into a new world.

These still pictures reached the homelands of most of the ten million
Jews alive at the time. Four in five of them were living in a ghetto or a
shtetl in the Russian Pale of Settlement or in Poland, partitioned between
the Empires of Germany, Russia and Hapsburg Austro-Hungary. After
the pogroms began in Odessa in 1871, a mass migration began to the west.
Within the next forty years, two million Jews left Russia for Poland and
Germany on the way toward the images of promise from America. Among
these emigrants from Middle Europe were the families of the founders of
the American film industry, Louis B. Mayer and the Schenck brothers
from Minsk and Lewis J. Zeleznik (or Selznick) from Kiev, Samuel
Goldfish (or Goldwyn) from Warsaw and the Warner brothers from nearby
Krasmaskhilz, Adolph Zukor and William Fox from the small towns of
Hapsburg Hungary, and their many cousins and relations. They would
eventually become the arbiters of the new moving pictures of America that
could be seen at nickelodeons and in penny arcades, then in adapted
theaters and picture palaces and cinemas. Their standards were those that
might please the American people and all nations. "You must be like a tea-
taster," declared the founder of the Hollywood studios, Adolph Zukor.
"Above all, you have to know the public, which I have studied from the

very first day I opened a nickelodeon. I pondered audience reaction every day. My major concern was to learn what they liked and what they didn't like, what gave them pleasure and what didn't."

By 1910, there were some ten thousand nickelodeons in the United States of America. They showed one- or two-reel films from eight in the morning continuously until midnight. By the outbreak of the First World War, there were as many nickelodeons spread across Europe. Silent moving images of a different life overseas now illuminated the eyes of the world and sent their messages abroad to those who wished to sail to America. Charles Chaplin, himself an immigrant, was the clown and messiah of the coming age of war and poverty and dislocation. His early films showed in the cities and towns of Middle Europe, also in the nickelodeons and cinemas of Jaroslaw, a Galician market town of thirty thousand inhabitants on the borders of Russia. It stood in the center of a triangle made by the Polish cities of Krakow, Lvov and Lublin, and was a prosperous place. Money flowed from the oilfields developing in nearby Borislav, the Baku of Poland, and from the famous yearly fair, the largest in Middle Europe other than Leipzig. Three hundred thousand traders and visitors used to crowd into the town and throng the Warsawski and the city hotels on Grunwaldzka Street and pour into the market square, dominated by its old town hall and the Orsetti Palace, built in the style of the Polish Renaissance. The ancient trade routes from the Baltic to the Black Sea and to the Levant passed through Jaroslaw: amber, furs and salt fish coming from the north: coral, cotton, tobacco and spices from the south.

Jewish families comprised nearly half of the town's population, some of them refugees from the frequent pogroms in the Russian Pale. One of them was the family of the tobacco merchant Simon Spiegel, his surname imposed upon him by German officials. He preferred studying the Talmud to wholesaling tobacco, but his determined wife, Regina, the daughter of a farmer from Bukovina in Romania, insisted on his earning a living. She was extremely Orthodox in her faith. To the Spiegels, a second son, Samuel, was born on the eleventh of November, 1901. Their hopes were set on the firstborn son, Shalom, who was to take his doctorate in medieval philosophy at the University of Vienna, and become a professor in the United States and in Israel, a theologian and a rabbi. Shalom was the obedient and studious child, but the younger Samuel was born stubborn and in his brother's shadow. He would grow to feel betrayed by his mother who, indeed, loved his brother more than him. He was to become what he always called himself, the black sheep of the family.

The boy Samuel liked to flee from the constrictions of the home and the prayerhouse. His mother was strict and domineering, something of a tartar who always reminded her husband that she was born a cut above him. Her sons were in awe of her, but Samuel was always running off to the traders in the market square and to the forbidden amusements of the penny arcades. He also escaped into the picture palace that showed the moving images of America, which began to fill his dreams. The cinema was not approved by the boy's rabbis, but it was the shortest way out of Galicia and the hot summers. In the words of Bruno Schulz from the nearby town of Drogobych, "After the fantastic adventures of the film, one's beating heart could calm down in the bright lobby, shut off from the impact of the great pathetic night; in that safe shelter, where time stood still, the light bulbs emitted waves of sterile light in a rhythm set by the dull rumbling of the projector, and kept by the shake of the cashier's box."

In the towns of southern Galicia, the Klondike of the black gold of oil destroyed the old patriarchal communities. Commercial values and false Americanization and the chance of turning a quick buck by dubious methods were transforming the old quarters from the nostalgic Cinnamon Shops beloved by Bruno Schulz into the Street of Crocodiles, repulsive and fascinating with its loose habits, many tongues and easy morals. There was no permanence anymore in society, and little continuity. Hundreds of thousands of Jews were pouring over the borders, fleeing from Russian persecution on their way to the West. Two million refugees left Galicia in the twenty-five years before the outbreak of the First World War, four hundred thousand in 1913 alone. Another chronicler of the end of the Hapsburg Empire, Joseph Roth, set many of his novels in Zlotograd, a fictional town on the Russian border. Near there, Jadlowker's border tavern was always open to assist deserters and refugees wanting to take ship to North America. Its location made it a town of migrants passing through the settled Jewish community. Jaroslaw was the same, and its streets resounded with all the tongues of Central Europe.

Although he was not distinguished in his studies at the local school, Samuel Spiegel showed an early gift for languages. At home, he spoke Yiddish, but in the markets, a knowledge of German, Polish and Russian was necessary. For Jaroslaw was on the frontier of four cultures, the vernacular Jewish language, and those of the great powers occupying Poland. Only at Hebrew did Samuel not excel. To him, it seemed a dead language, fit only for rabbis. Yet his older brother, Shalom, pursued his studies in theology as if called to them. In reaction, Samuel rebelled against the rituals of the Sabbath, the rules of diet and hygiene, the black clothes and the hair curls, and the arranged marriages of adolescents. What his brother was, he would not be.

Although the capitalist markets, cinemas and dreams of America excited the young Samuel, two other avenues of liberation beckoned him, revolutionary socialism and Zionism. Jews were prominent among the Bolsheviks, although Leon (Bronstein) Trotsky opposed Zionism, saying, "I am a revolutionary, not a Jew." But many of the Jewish socialist revolutionaries also supported Zionism and the colonization of Palestine. The Zionist leader Chaim Weizmann himself came from the small Russian town of Motol near Minsk before he emigrated to Britain to become a professor of chemistry, specializing in the manufacture of explosives. Hundreds of Socialist and Zionist clubs sprang up in the towns of Poland and the Russian Pale and influenced rebellious young minds like that of Samuel Spiegel. As one prewar leaflet from Lvov declared:

> *We see before us two great and powerful movements: socialism which seeks to liberate us from economic and political slavery; and Zionism which seeks to liberate us from the yoke of Diaspora. . . . Both promise us a glorious future.*

The saddest day of his life, Samuel Spiegel often said, was the day he heard of the death of the Emperor Franz Josef, just as the happiest day of his life was to be the birth of the state of Israel. The emperor's death signaled the end of the Hapsburg Empire, which had shielded the Jewish settlements within its borders from pogrom and persecution. Galicia became a cockpit of the struggle between the great powers. Conflict swept across it for the four years of the First World War and the three years of the Bolshevik Revolution. To be Jewish on the Eastern marches in the second decade of the twentieth century was to be in the bloody birth of modern Europe.

Millions of the Jews in the East became refugees; more than a hundred thousand were killed, innocent civilians caught in the conflict, the victims of unruly soldiers or peasant pogroms. The Russians advanced against the Austrians and took Galicia; but Field Marshal von Mackensen counterattacked with German armies, took back Galicia and pressed on to capture Warsaw and Wilno. The retreating Russians scorched the earth, burned whole villages, dismantled factories, fired oil wells at Borislav and deported a million peasants to work as forced laborers. None of the three great powers valued the Jews as fighting men: conscription into alien armies was not their fate or their future.

Yet one week in 1917 and two events changed their possibilities forever. Arthur Balfour, the British foreign secretary, made his declaration that Palestine would be treated as a homeland for the Jews: it was being taken from the Turks by General Allenby, assisted by Lawrence of Arabia: Chaim Weizmann would soon lead a Zionist commission to Jerusalem to prepare for immigration. Then, five days after the Balfour Declaration, the Bolsheviks seized power in Russia and a revolutionary war began. Initially, the radical Jews in Eastern Europe supported the Bolsheviks, who appeared to offer equality and liberty to the ghettos of the East. Three of Lenin's closest advisers were Jewish— Zinoviev, Kamenev and Trotsky. But Lenin opposed Zionism as a separatist movement: he wanted the total assimilation of the Russian Jews into the motherland. Several thousand Zionists were sent to camps in Siberia, from which only dozens returned alive. To Simon Spiegel, an idealist Zionist and a supporter of Weizmann, Bolshevism was a threat. But Palestine might become the promised land of refuge, where the Spiegels and other Zionist families might build a spiritual home.

At the end of the First World War, Galicia was left to starvation and anarchy. It was awash with refugees and deserters, worse off than ravaged Belgium. Violence and plundering were directed particularly at the Jewish communities. The new armies raised by Marshal Pilsudski to create and defend an independent Poland treated the Jews as aliens more suspect than Ukrainians or Russians or Germans. Attacks on the ghettos were encouraged as the soldiers stood by. The pogroms that took place in the two years of struggle between the new Polish state and the Bolshevik Red armies were worse than any under the czar or the Austrian emperor. The Poles made an alliance with Hetman Petlyura and his White armies seeking an independent Ukraine. They advanced as far as Kiev, before being routed by the Red armies. Now it was the turn of the Bolsheviks to advance on Warsaw. Isaac Babel rode with the Cossacks through Galicia and despised his fellow Jews from Poland just as much as the Viennese did. He found them backward and uncouth and warped, men with long bony backs and tragic yellow beards. He admired his Cossacks as noble savages, even if they did hate Jews and barely tolerated him. Blood and murder, violence and death were Babel's world of wandering war. As he wrote of the cemetery of the little Jewish town of Kazin, where a burial vault enclosed four generations of rabbis, the last one, Azrael, killed by the Cossacks, the memorial stone had the eloquence of a Bedouin's prayer.

Azrael son of Ananias, Jehova's mouthpiece.
Elijah son of Azrael, brain that struggled single-handed with oblivion.
Wolff son of Elijah, prince robbed from the Torah in his nineteenth spring.
Judah son of Wolff, Rabbi of Kracow and Prague.
O death, O covetous one, O greedy thief, why couldst thou not have spared us, just for once?

Death spared Samuel Spiegel in Galicia. He was kept at home when soldiers or marauders swept through Jaroslaw. He was sent briefly to the gymnasium of the neighboring city of Lvov, but it was no safer. He learned to fight as a young Jew and an outcast, an alien in a land he had thought was his own. There was a pogrom in Lvov in November 1918, followed by massacres in the ghettos of Wilno and Pinsk. Fearful that their sons would be drafted into a forced-labor gang or killed in the aimless current violence, the Spiegels decided to abandon their possessions in Jaroslaw and flee with millions of others to Vienna in 1919. They might be poor, but they could perhaps have Shalom educated at the great university there.

The Spiegels found living space in the Jewish Quarter of the Austrian capital at 31 Mosergasse. Their few resources were spent on finding a place for Shalom in the university and for Samuel in the local gymnasium. Samuel was later to claim that he followed his older brother to the university, where he studied economics and languages and drama. It was untrue, but he did learn to speak fluent German with a Polish accent, and to play football and tennis. It was another betrayal. The pretense which he maintained throughout his adult life that he held a Viennese degree indicated the value he placed on the higher education he never had. His university was the university of life and hard knocks, his syllabus was the syllabus of survival and independence. He learned to avoid wars and taxes, to disbelieve governments and stability, to trust only in money and himself. Whatever natural qualities he had as a boy, he became a stubborn rebel as a young man, determined to break away from his family and his past. He could not get to America to check on the moving pictures of prosperity there. Instead, he determined to go to Palestine, where his father had his Zionist friends and where socialist communities promised a new life. Traveling on Polish documents, he left as a Young Pioneer to test the truth of the ideals of a promised land and a national home.

CHAPTER TWO

False Starts

Well, professor, I have proved a theory of relatives too
—don't hire them.

JACK WARNER to ALBERT EINSTEIN

Samuel Spiegel arrived in Palestine as part of the third *Aliya*, the wave of thirty-five thousand refugees from Eastern Europe who were fleeing the aftermath of the European war. He found Jaffa a small port of oriental squalor, where two thousand Jews lived among eight thousand Arabs, under a British administration. The little city offered no chance for a decent job. But out in the Valley of Jezreel, which meant "where God will sow," immigrants from Russia and Poland were setting up new communities. The cost of clearing the swamps was high, as the successful colony at Hedera had already proved. There two hundred of the five hundred original settlers had died of the fever in the process of draining the land and making the marsh bloom like a rose.

In spite of the conditions, Samuel Spiegel went to the Jezreel Valley to join a kibbutz there, a society without property or greed. With mattocks and spades, scythes and pruning-hooks, a new Garden of Israel was being planted. Spiegel lived in tents with the other Pioneers. Luxury was a sheet of plywood to keep one's blanket off the soggy ground. Necessities were rags to bind around one's feet when shoes wore out. There was little food until the first harvests were gathered. "We had nothing," Golda Meir from Kiev and Pinsk remembered of her days as a Young Pioneer. "There was nothing to eat."

Spiegel himself suffered and starved as he dug ditches and sewers in the marshes. His years of labor were later amended in his publicity material as a film producer to serving as a drainage expert, reclaiming land and assisting in the exploitation of the Dead Sea. The hard work developed his powerful, short body until his broad shoulders seemed to support his enormous head as surely as a battlement on the wall of a Crusader castle. His fine nose, sharp as an eagle's beak, stood on a face of heavy distinction. Over large and brilliant eyes, his lids drooped easily in circumspection, while his tongue flicked at thin lips that would stutter nervously. His little legs did not detract from a powerful presence that seemed to challenge his poverty and lack of opportunity. He learned English, the language of those who occupied Palestine and America.

He returned to Vienna in 1922 to visit his family. His brother, Shalom, had completed his historical and theological studies at the university. Shalom had also become a leader of the Zionist Youth movement, and the whole Spiegel family had decided to emigrate to Palestine, where Samuel had led the way. But back at Mosergasse, Samuel met a young Canadian Rachel "Ray" Agronovich, a year older than he was, but also on her way to Palestine with the Spiegels to assist in the building of the Zionist dream. He courted her, his father approved the match and he married her. He had no prospects except for the life of the Pioneer camps, but that was what she seemed to want.

In Palestine, the Spiegel family went its various ways. Shalom found work in biblical research and teaching medieval Hebrew literature. He was, as his brother said, the white sheep of the family. The parents lived with Shalom in Jerusalem, where a Hebrew university was being founded: it was opened in 1925 in the presence of Chaim Weizmann, Lord Balfour of the Declaration, the liberator of the city, General Allenby, and Herbert Samuel, who was the first British High Commissioner of Palestine, a Zionist and a Jew. After the founding of the university, the Spiegels achieved their ambitions with the older son employed as a theologian and a historian in the ancient holy city of their faith.

In the camp communities in the swamplands, the younger Samuel Spiegel was losing his hopes of creating a new family in a new society. The terrible conditions imposed on the Pioneers were too much for his health. Frequent bouts of malaria sapped his energy and vigor. He moved to join his parents in Jerusalem, where his wife bore him a daughter, Alisa, in the fourth year of their marriage. Samuel had no degree, he could not teach or find work. He tried to make a living as a guide to tourists around Jerusalem, but it was not enough. He heard of an opportunity to become a broker in the expanding port of Tel Aviv, which had been a minor suburb of Jaffa, but was now becoming the first Jewish entrepôt in Palestine, particularly for the export of cotton from British-controlled Egypt to the textile mills of Europe. Spiegel claimed knowledge of the Polish market, based on his connections in Jaroslaw, and secured a commission to export cotton to Poland. He decided to return there, although he would have to abandon his wife and baby daughter only six months old. Feeling betrayed by his parents' love for his studious older brother, sickened by the deprivations of building a Garden of Israel, he decided to betray his own little family. He filed for divorce, broke with his relations, put socialism and Zionism behind him, and set off for his homeland, which had defeated the Red Army and become a haven for the refugee Jews of Eastern Europe, frustrated by new quota restrictions from migrating to America. There the Statue of Liberty seemed to be changed into what Sam Goldwyn miscalled "the statue of limitation." The chances of a Polish Jew becoming an American citizen had diminished.

Spiegel was not to see his wife or his daughter again for sixteen years, and little of his family. He reacted against the Orthodox Judaism of his brother and parents by becoming something of an atheist. He spurned Zionist experiments in socialism to become a stock promoter as well as a cotton broker. He traveled widely through the markets and cities of Central Europe, doing his deals and developing his gifts of persuasion and tongues. He could convince nearly anyone, particularly a woman, of anything, and he learned to speak the nine leading languages of Europe; only his Hebrew was still poor. He understood Czech and Slavic dialects, he spoke good Arabic and had a fair knowledge of Syrian and other Levantine languages. He developed a passion for the ballet and the theater to add to his boyhood love of the cinema.

Although Spiegel could not emigrate to the United States, he could travel there. He had met a few Americans in Palestine and Europe. Moreover, Poland was suffering from a recession, and business was poor. So Spiegel sailed to New York in 1927, soon to be followed by his divorced wife and small daughter, who were emigrating there from Palestine. Spiegel found few takers for cotton futures in New York and decided to travel to San Francisco to deal in the commodity. Unfortunately, he had no dollars and few American contacts. One of them, a young American whose father was a newspaper proprietor and banker in Louisville, Kentucky, was surprised one day to find Spiegel passing through his hometown. He had last met Spiegel in the King David Hotel in Jerusalem, a city that Spiegel had shown him in return for his address back home. Now Spiegel persuaded the banker father to cash a check for $150, which was later not honored. The banker was furious and was one of many who hunted Spiegel across the United States as he left a trail of bouncing checks behind him on his way to California.

In San Francisco, Spiegel also failed as a cotton broker. He continued to pass bad checks and hope in the future. He wanted to exploit his gift for languages and his knowledge of the European theater on the West Coast. For an upheaval in film technology had presented him with an opportunity to break into his dream factory, Hollywood. As its originator Adolph Zukor declared, "In 1926, sound pictures came in. In that revolution lies the whole business. If it hadn't been for an amplifier that the telephone company perfected, motion pictures would never have grown to be so important in the amusement world."

Zukor himself had no formal education, but with his Paramount Famous Lasky corporation, he held himself to be the *primum mobile* of motion pictures in New York and California. He claimed that the other new studios, Metro-Goldwyn-Mayer, Warner Brothers, Fox and Columbia, merely took his ideas. "They did everything but murder. I didn't raid anyone because I started the whole business. But I had something others could take." And take they did, Louis B. Mayer and Samuel Goldwyn, William Fox and Carl Laemmle, and particularly the Warner brothers, whose first sound pictures like *The Jazz Singer* were triumphs at the box office. Laemmle had known perfectly well that silent films spoke more widely than words could tell. In an early advertisement for his Universal Pictures he wrote:

> *Universal Pictures speak the Universal language. Universal stories told in pictures need no translation, no interpreter. Regardless of creed, color, race or nationality, everyone in the universe understands the stories that are told by Universal Pictures.*

Motion pictures were universal, tongues were not. When sound could be applied to moving images and silent films could speak, a fearful babble of different languages assaulted the common screen. Once mime had made up for lack of speech and sparse translated titles had carried the message everywhere. But in this new revolution of voices, screenplays had to contain dialogue, although the action sequences were hardly altered. Playwrights were in demand rather than screenwriters. Theater directors displaced film directors. Voice coaches flourished under false pretenses, as in Kaufman and Hart's play *Once in a Lifetime*. And there was the question of the foreign market. Sound pictures would have to be translated into foreign languages and alien voices dubbed onto the sound tracks. Even Charlie Chaplin would have to seem to speak in French, German, Italian, Polish and

Russian. "The one problem that worried everybody," Zukor's production manager Walter Wanger recalled, "was what the hell are we to do with the foreign market." He himself made his studio's first sound picture in six weeks, when Zukor said he would kiss Wanger's ass in Macy's window if he could do it.

Hollywood producers were looking for people with Spiegel's skills. Many Central Europeans with a knowledge of languages and the theater were coming to California, but not all of them were gifted. At Metro-Goldwyn-Mayer, one of Irving Thalberg's leading production assistants, the brilliant and neurotic Paul Bern, was searching for an aide. He himself had written scripts for the directors Ernst Lubitsch and Josef von Sternberg, but he needed more material from Europe. He was pressed for time, as he was appointed the supervisor of most of the Greta Garbo pictures.

In his later promotion of himself, Spiegel claimed that Bern had discovered him at the University of California at Berkeley, where he had been asked to deliver a course of lectures on European drama. He had no qualifications to do so. His claim was good publicity, but poor history. Once he had repudiated his family and his past in Poland and Palestine, Spiegel began to invent his origins daily. The creation of a changing story about his early life was designed to obscure unpleasant facts and impress future supporters. The fiction was bound to succeed when there was no one to contradict him. Fortunately for Spiegel's later legend, Paul Bern had suicidal tendencies. He attempted to kill himself on the marriage of the beautiful Barbara La Marr to an Irish actor after she had already refused to wed him because of his sexual failings. When he did eventually marry the alluring Jean Harlow, who was half his age and the sex symbol of America, he achieved the suicide he had tried before. He shot himself in front of Harlow's bedroom mirror, while she was playing *Red Dust* with Clark Gable. He left her a note confessing to the frightful wrong he had done her and to his abject humiliation. His last night with Harlow—he wrote—was only a comedy.

Whatever the truth of Spiegel's meeting with the unstable Bern, it is certain that Bern hired him as a special adviser on European plays that might make film properties for sound pictures. Spiegel read original stories in French, German, Polish, Spanish and Italian, and recommended subjects to Bern. Their relationship did not flourish. Spiegel was too successful with young women for his master's temperament. He was soon fired, but found himself another job at Universal translating American film dialogue into French and German and other European languages. He made friends with two other immigrants to America who worked at Universal, the director William Wyler and the producer Paul Kohner, both of whom had graduated from shipping clerks and managers of foreign publicity for Carl Laemmle in New York to makers of motion pictures in California. Wyler was actually one of Laemmle's cousins, a genuine member of the foreign legion of Laemmle relatives employed at Universal, while Kohner passed for Uncle Carl's nephew. Laemmle always ignored Jack Warner's Theory of Relatives—"Don't hire them."

For Universal as for the other studios, Manhattan remained the center for financing and distributing feature films, while Hollywood was the production center. The pictures made on the West Coast were financed and sold by the East Coast, and there were running battles between them. As Walter Wanger observed, "Films were considered a third-class operation. Bankers weren't interested. Neither were writers. You couldn't hire actors from the theater. They looked down on pictures." Hollywood itself was parochial. "There's nothing worldly about the community. They're all anxious for social status." But New York was a metropolis with a more cosmopolitan point of view, a much more civilized attitude. The heads of the studios, Zukor and Laemmle and Goldwyn, who had an office larger than Mussolini's ballroom, had to commute by train across the continent to settle the differences of East and West, which were often matters of language, the field where Spiegel was hired to advise. On one occasion, Zukor objected that the first Mae West movie was being advertised as "Hitting the high spot of lusty entertainment." On being told that "lusty" derived from the German word *lustig*, meaning life and energy and vigor, Zukor replied that he did not need a Harvard education. "When I look at that dame's tits, I know what lusty means."

In such a lusty world, Spiegel thrived, even if he was not accepted by the German-speaking colony that was carving out its place in Hollywood. Although the two "Vons," Stroheim and Sternberg, had caused difficulties with the studios because of their autocratic manners and strange tastes in film subjects, Ernst Lubitsch, the son of a Berlin tailor, had become the master director of romantic sexual comedy after the success in 1924 of *The Marriage Circle*, its script adapted by Paul Bern from a play by Lothar Schmidt. Lubitsch was witty and charming: he looked to William Wyler like a combination of Napoleon and Punchinello. He assimilated well into Hollywood life and his home on Sunday afternoons was the prized meeting-place of the expatriate German-speaking colony. Then a *salon* rose for refugees to the film city, run by the wife of another German director, Berthold Viertel, who had arrived with his Salka, an actress discovered by the great impresario Max Reinhardt. Like Spiegel, Salka Viertel had been born in small-town Galicia and educated in Lvov, but she became a catalyst to the German-speaking intellectuals who were arriving in increasing numbers in California.

Spiegel's brother, Shalom, came to America in 1928 to become a professor and librarian at the Jewish Institute of Religion in New York and then the William Prager professor of medieval Hebrew literature at the Jewish Theological Seminary. The arrival of the white sheep of the family signaled the departure of the black sheep. Samuel Spiegel was charged in San Francisco for issuing a series of bad checks, dating from his arrival in the United States and his failure as a cotton broker. After a plea bargain, he was convicted in 1929 for issuing one bad check for ten dollars and was sentenced to nine months' imprisonment in the county jail. He served five months and was paroled for four months before he was deported, in 1930, back to his native Poland.

His conviction, which implied moral turpitude, seemed to have destroyed any chance of entering America again. He could never acquire a work permit or a passport. It had taken William Wyler eight years of residence and a clean record to acquire his American passport. But Paul Kohner had become Carl Laemmle's roving ambassador and head of European production, and he was looking for a man of many languages and skills to recut and dub Universal films for European distribution. Remembering Spiegel's ability in his Hollywood days, Kohner located him in Poland and recalled him to Berlin in 1930 to do the job. Berlin was then a city of Berliners, refugees and deportees—cosmopolitan, decadent and ambiguous. After William Wyler had made his film *Hell's Heroes*, he was sent by Universal to Berlin to give a press conference organized by Spiegel at the Eden Hotel, crowned by its enclosed roof garden. Wyler found a whirlpool of people with nothing to lose but paper money. "It was tango and rain falling on the glass roof and every night a different girl."

It was also the Berlin in which the Nazis were rising to power. Year by year, they grew to dominate the streets and the government. Even before Adolf Hitler became chancellor and Dr. Goebbels imposed Nazi censorship, German film distributors were worried about threats of riots if certain foreign pictures were shown. Spiegel's chief problem lay with Universal's flagship production of *All Quiet on the Western Front*, Lewis Milestone's version of Remarque's novel about the futility of war. Milestone had been born in Odessa in Russia and raised in Bessarabia before emigrating to America. He was no friend of useless slaughter. He tried many climaxes to Remarque's novel, but could only end with the original version, the death of the hero, shot by a lone sniper while reaching out for a butterfly on an empty beer can on a day so quiet that the official report read, "All quiet on the Western Front." The picture flouted all the rules by not ending in a crescendo. "You have to have a diminuendo," Milestone said. "You cannot top the whole piece." The Nazis thought it decadent and unpatriotic, but for unknown reasons the Reich Film Censorship Board passed it for public showing. At its Berlin premiere the Nazis caused a riot. They released thousands of white mice and exploded tear gas and stink bombs. Three members of the audience were killed and twenty-two injured before the police arrived to restore order.

The film was now banned by the Censorship Board as a provocation to riot. Its showing became a test of Nazi strength in democratic Germany. The prime minister and liberal leaders convened a special session of the Reichstag to discuss the film. At the time, one in six members of the Reichstag was a Nazi. In hundreds of screenings, Spiegel had shown the film to individual politicians including the Nazi leaders, Goebbels and Göring and Röhm. He was even protected from Nazi retaliation by a squad of four secret policemen. When the vote was taken in December 1931, on screening *All Quiet on the Western Front* throughout Germany, the Nazis marched out of the Reichstag in a military formation singing the Horst Wessel song and raising their clenched fists toward Spiegel in the public gallery as a warning of what was to come. But the vote was in favor of the showing of the film in Germany.

Spiegel also worked on the Italian version of the film in 1931 and showed it privately to Mussolini in the projection room of the International Film Institute built by Erpi in the Duce's Villa Venezia. "Mussolini," Spiegel recalled, "surprisingly, liked the film. After it was done, he congratulated Universal and me, and said it was the greatest film he had ever seen." But the powerful message for peace was hardly what Mussolini wanted. The next day, the film was banned without the right of appeal throughout Italy. It was, however, shown in all other European countries and by Spiegel personally to the World Disarmament Conference delegates in Geneva. Its message of peace was widespread.

While working for Universal, Spiegel managed to raise the money for a low-budget motion picture that he produced, *Marriage Unlimited*. Its script was excellent, its unknown actors unusual, its direction poor; but it did make a profit and gave Spiegel a reputation in Berlin. He followed this success with three failed productions, including *The Unhappy Mr. Five*—starring the popular opera singer Billy Dongraf-Fassbinder, whose family was later to produce a famous German director. Spiegel asked Rudi Fehr, the son of a prominent German banker and a film financier at UFA, the leading production company, to edit his pictures, for he had an eye on the father's resources as well as the young man's talent.

Yet Spiegel was a minor figure in the German film scene. *The Universal Filmlexicon* of 1932 did not mention him or Paul Kohner. It bore articles by Goldwyn and Laemmle, complaining that the conversion of the industry to talking pictures had cost three hundred million dollars, only to be followed by the worldwide depression and a slump in moviegoing. Yet good talkies were a business proposition. The leading German film producer Erich Pommer agreed. Paradoxically, the international appeal of the silent film had not yet been replaced by the speaking film because of its national limitations. A common language of the talking screen was still being discovered. Its success depended on writers with an international appeal and good translators. *The Filmlexicon* praised Samuel "Billie" Wilder as the best of the new screenwriters: his collaboration on *Menschen am Sonntag* of 1929 with Robert and Curt Siodmak and Fred Zinnemann had shown his faculty of raising into the sphere of art the ordinary things which others hardly noticed. Wilder knew Spiegel in Berlin, but had decided to flee the city for Paris when Hitler became chancellor and the Reichstag burned. "It seemed," Wilder said later, "the wise thing to do."

Spiegel soon arrived at the same decision. One of Hitler's first acts as chancellor was to ban all showings of *All Quiet on the Western Front*. Spiegel himself was in certain danger. Although he was preparing to begin another film, *Invisible Opponents*, he decided that he had to leave the country for Austria on the Saturday of the Reichstag fire, the third of March, 1933. As he told the story:

I got up late that day, and went around the corner to my barber to get a shave. While he was shaving me the barber whispered, "Don't go home tonight." That was sufficient warning. Without a hat, and with only a few marks in my pocket, I walked out of the barber shop and went directly to the station without returning home. The banks were closed that day, so I couldn't stop to get money. The train for Vienna crossed the Austrian border at two A.M. *of the following morning. At six* A.M. *the borders were closed forever—and thereafter nobody left Germany without the permission and knowledge of the Gestapo.... At one* A.M., *while my train was still inside Germany, my house was surrounded by fifty Nazis. They broke in and smashed everything I owned. They wouldn't believe my aged Catholic housekeeper when she said she didn't know where I was, and so they beat her so badly that she spent months thereafter in the hospital. My barber had been a member of that troop.*

Spiegel often told the story of his escape. In one version, he fled with the actor Oscar Homolka, changing trains to avoid detection, and arrived in Vienna with only four marks, a toothbrush and a film script for Homolka to play for him in Austria. In yet another version, Spiegel's barber drove his Cord coupé and his clothes to Austria before returning to Nazi duties. Spiegel always embroidered the tapestry of his past, but as he said, it was lucky that unpleasant things were "obliterated by some kind of providential gift of forgetting." However he left Germany, he did leave in the nick of time. And he always made the same comment on his decision: "These are the accidents of history that prevent you from becoming a lampshade."

CHAPTER THREE

A Guest of His Majesty's Government

Our comedies are not to be laughed at.

SAM GOLDWYN

Arriving in Vienna with his script, Spiegel tried to produce it. *Invisible Opponents* was a story about swindles in the oil industry: there had been such crooks in Jaroslaw. Spiegel formed Pan Films and persuaded the largest company in Vienna, Sascha-Film Industrie, to coproduce his scenario in two languages for wider distribution. The German actors included Oscar Homolka, the French ones Arlette Marshall, while Peter Lorre played in both versions. Spiegel summoned Rudi Fehr from Berlin to cut the picture: Fehr's family was Jewish as well as rich, and he was glad to leave. While there were Austrian Nazis parading up and down the streets of Vienna, they did not yet dominate the government. The shooting of the film went well, except that Spiegel occasionally failed to pay the technicians every Friday. Fehr noticed that he always received his wages on time, while the others often had to wait. He asked Spiegel the reason why. "You know you get paid every week," Spiegel said. "It proves I'm honest. When your father's ready to finance the picture, you know where to send him."

While Spiegel may not have paid all his technicians regularly, he lived well. He had his large Cord coupé and competed with the director Otto Preminger for the favors of Hedy Kiesler, later known as Hedy Lamarr. Spiegel would take her out to the Döblinger Bad and the Femina: the Austrian film producer Franz Antel remembers a real love story between the two of them. Hedy was already married to a rich munitions manufacturer, who was furious about her nude bathing scenes and simulated orgasm in *Ecstasy*, but she was unfaithful to him and restless. Vienna was no place to be for those who did not support the Nazis. With the assassination of the Austrian chancellor Dollfuss, a swing to the anti-Semitic right was inevitable, an invasion by Hitler probable. Hollywood beckoned the ambitious Lamarr as it did Preminger, who had already been offered a job at Twentieth Century–Fox. Spiegel had his car and his Polish passport,

Otto Preminger had a roll of Austrian banknotes worth seven thousand dollars and an Austrian passport. They set off for Paris and the future in 1935. There were strict regulations against the export of currency, and they were bound to be searched. As they approached the frontier, Preminger kept on putting the banknotes in the pocket of Spiegel's leather coat with an astrakhan collar, while Spiegel kept returning the money. At last, Preminger lost his temper. He was paying for the trip. Spiegel had to carry the cash. He put the roll of notes for the last time in Spiegel's pocket. At the frontier, the two passports were checked. Both had Jewish names, but Preminger's father had been attorney-general in Vienna, while Spiegel was an obscure Pole. Spiegel was hauled out and strip-searched. Preminger sweated in agony until Spiegel's return. Spiegel did not say a word, but drove over the border to safety. "Where's the money?" Preminger demanded. "Did they take it?" Spiegel smiled and said, "It's in your pocket. I put it back. Because you they won't search." In the many versions of the escape story told variously by Spiegel and Preminger, each claimed that the other was stripped and searched. Spiegel had the last word, however, asserting that he had bribed the border guards with a thousand-dollar Confederate bank note, worth precisely nothing.

In Paris, Spiegel and Preminger found that many German-speaking Jewish refugees were competing for jobs in the French film industry. The producers Erich Pommer and Seymour Nebenzal had fled there—their productions had included *Menschen am Sonntag* and *M* with Peter Lorre. They preferred to employ in their French productions such distinguished refugees as the half-Jewish director Fritz Lang, who had fled after Dr. Goebbels had summoned him to say that Hitler had seen *Metropolis*, had declared that Lang would make *the* Nazi picture and wanted him to lead the German film industry. Soaked with sweat, Lang had gone from Germany that evening with a runaway fund of a thousand dollars. In Paris, he made Ferenc Molnár's *Liliom* for Pommer and French Fox, before being recruited for Metro-Goldwyn-Mayer by David Selznick. Wilder, who now called himself Billy, managed to have a script made called *Mauvaise Graine*, and to sell another script called *Pam-Pam* to Columbia Pictures, which earned him a contract for six months and a ticket across the Atlantic, although he had to spend a time of waiting in Mexico to satisfy American immigration quota requirements. Even when he arrived in Hollywood, he "kind of starved for a little bit." He shared a room with Peter Lorre, who claimed, "We lived on a can of soup a day." Otto

Preminger, who had already made contact with Twentieth Century–Fox, sailed for the United States. Spiegel, however, had no luck except in running errands for Seymour Nebenzal. He had been forced to sell his coupé, and so he had to take the train and the boat across the English Channel to try his fortune in London, where he arrived with little more than the suit on his back.

As always, Spiegel had his contacts and his charm, and now had a minor reputation earned in Berlin and in Vienna. He walked into the office of the film producer Joseph J. Bamberger, who took him under his wing. Spiegel told his story of how the barber had advised him to flee from Berlin and how he had worked for anti-Nazi youth groups. Bamberger lent him an apartment at Elstree, and Spiegel quickly established himself in the film industry and with wealthy and influential people including Kathleen, Countess of Drogheda. She taught him some of the refinements of English style and introduced him to other British aristocrats. He won over a wealthy young man, Laurence Evans, who was associated with Bamberger and had cash to spare. He also appealed to rich young men about town such as Marcus Sieff, who remembered lending him money and never being recompensed and said, "He never paid bills as a matter of principle."

Now a leading agent, Laurence Evans, who had inherited money, saw himself as someone with a passion for making films. With Spiegel, he floated a company, the British and Continental Film Corporation Limited, with offices in Lower Regent Street. He took Spiegel to his tailors, Hawes and Curtis, to set him up in decent suits, which Spiegel, like any English gentleman, did not pay for. Dazzled by Spiegel's cosmopolitan knowledge and command of languages, the young Evans was persuaded to go to Paris for the weekend to meet the silent comic star Buster Keaton, then filming *Le Roi des Champs-Elysées* in between bouts with the demon drink which he usually lost. The two men stayed at the Ritz in a suite with two bedrooms. On the Saturday, Spiegel arranged two girls for the afternoon. "I speak the language," he said magnanimously. "I will settle everything." But on the Golden Arrow back to Boulogne, Spiegel introduced his young patron to gin rummy and by the time they were on the cross-Channel ferry, Evans had lost the price of Spiegel's girls and the rooms at the Ritz. He had paid for Spiegel's jaunt to Paris.

The trip abroad was not wasted. Buster Keaton, saddled with debts and a fading reputation, agreed to star in Spiegel's first English film, variously entitled, *The Gentleman*, *The Intruder* and *The Invader*. Based on a story told by Keaton, the script was written by Edwin Greenwood, the author of a popular thirties novel, *Love on the Dole*. The plot was thin. Keaton was to act Leander Proudfoot, a wealthy yacht-owner who has moored his boat in a small Spanish port; attracted to a Spanish girl, played by Paul Kohner's wife, Lupita Tovar, Keaton is used as a patsy to solve her problems with her two lovers. During the writing of the script, Spiegel intervened constantly, although his command of English and film language was still imperfect. During a row at two in the morning between him, the screenwriter and the film's director, Adrian Brunel, Spiegel was accused of being offensive. He admitted that he was, but added, "Films which run smoothly are colorless. Only films which are produced in strife have any outstanding merit."

Spiegel's problem was that the film was underfinanced. Although Keaton was only getting $12,000 (£3,000) to play the lead, and although the full budget was only $120,000 (£30,000), Spiegel did not have it. Through his aristocratic friends, he had met the lawyer of the eccentric Sir Francis Cook, one of the richest men in England and a patron of the arts. The lawyer got Cook to agree to use some of his fortune to finance *The Invader*, which had begun shooting. Unfortunately, Spiegel was overspending his producer's expenses by staying at the Dorchester Hotel and running an open house for his friends, who included the young John Huston, so penniless in London that he was sleeping on the Embankment and living in Hyde Park while trying to concoct a script to pay his way abroad. "One can't evade a bad streak," Huston recalled. "You have to pull your way through it. There's no such thing as asking for help."

Yet Spiegel was helping Huston, although he was not paying him for writing a script about a Scots gangster which, incredibly, was meant to star Emil Jannings. Spiegel and Huston used to dine at a small restaurant in Mayfair where the film expense account also paid the bills. Huston saw a beautiful woman sitting at another table with a man and Maurice Chevalier. He scrawled a caricature of her on the paper cloth and delivered it to her, followed by Spiegel. They were trying to charm the woman away to their table, when to his horror, Spiegel discovered that the unknown man was his financier, Sir Francis Cook. He was begging Chevalier to play the lead in *The Invader*, rather than Keaton, while the beautiful woman was Lady Cook. At that encounter, Spiegel compromised his film's finance, but he used his hypnotic charm on Lady Cook to such effect that she became his lifelong friend with total faith in his genius.

The filming was going badly. The director Adrian Brunel's difficulties with his colleagues involved "financial recklessness, writing phoney cheques, police charges, lack of sexual control, and other disturbing addictions." Although Spiegel had a note given to Brunel on set about Keaton—"DON'T LET HIM DRINK"—Keaton drank so much he could hardly get out a word. The cameraman was Eugen Schüfftan, another émigré from Central Europe who had worked for Spiegel on *Invisible Opponents*, but who shot the bright, light comedy in the dark atmospheric tones of German expressionism, as if the Costa Brava were enclosed in the cabinet of Dr. Caligari. Even a routine with a troupe of dancing girls who could not dance looked like a mating ritual for cave bears and wasted a fifth of the total budget. As for exterior shots, the sound-track was punctuated by pneumatic drills. An underground railroad was being built beside the studio.

Everything that could go wrong went wrong. Brunel advised his producer that he could not shoot enough material to make a film that would run for the seventy-five minutes Spiegel had contracted to deliver. Once he lost his temper with Spiegel and being a man who rarely lost his temper, he was immediately ashamed, but Spiegel was delighted. It was a technique of his dominance as a film producer, even when he did not yet know much about film production. He liked to provoke confrontations and prove his power by forgiving the outburst. "You were grand this afternoon, Adrian," he told Brunel. "I always thought you were a great director."

His charm and magnanimity did not extend to paying Brunel his full fee: the director only received a third of what he was due because Spiegel had run out of money during the shooting. Sir Francis Cook had instructed his lawyer to trim the budget. He was no longer prepared to subsidize Spiegel's extravagance in one of London's best hotels, so Spiegel left the Dorchester for modest lodgings, but he began issuing worthless checks and guarantees in order to complete the editing of the film. A lucky encounter with Rudi Fehr in a bottle club in London gave Spiegel a cheap editor, but one without a visa. Fehr had to be sent to France in order to be readmitted to England with the labor permit that Spiegel had fixed for him.

Fehr had his problems in making the final cut of the film. Brunel had been right, and his edited version only ran for five reels and sixty minutes instead of the six reels and seventy-five minutes that Spiegel had promised. From the footage left on the cutting-room floor, Fehr had to recut the film to meet its contractual length. In the final version, when a door was banged shut, it stayed shut on the screen for several seconds. Then Keaton was seen on the far side of the door, still shutting it before dashing off about his business. This was the only comedy in the film, and it was all unintentional. "It was a disaster," Spiegel's young associate Laurence Evans said. "Buster Keaton should not speak."

Spiegel's bad checks finally bounced back at him. He was arrested for incurring debts by false pretenses, obtaining money by means of worthless checks and forging a guarantee. That same week, Carl Laemmle sold the bankrupt Universal Pictures: the *Kinematograph Weekly* printed both items of news on its front page. Released on bail, Spiegel was committed for trial at the Central Criminal Court at the Old Bailey on April 8, 1936. Instead of going to court, he threw a lavish champagne and caviar party for his wealthier friends and associates at the Dorchester. During the occasion, two police officers arrived to take him in charge. As he was led away, he showed generosity and style. "Ladies and gentlemen," he declared, "please continue to be my guests. I am temporarily the guest of His Majesty's Government."

Laurence Evans was present at the Old Bailey, where Spiegel was sentenced to three months' imprisonment to be followed by deportation. It was the end of the British and Continental Film Corporation, particularly as *The Invader* failed both in England and in the United States, where it was called *An Old Spanish Custom*. "The day has passed," Buster Keaton recalled, "when the public would come to see a movie with inferior props, camera work, and generally poor production."

While he was out on bail, Spiegel had been on the verge of a deal with the leading British literary figure, George Bernard Shaw. He had borrowed all of Lady Cook's signed first editions of Shaw's works, and had approached the great man for permission to film them. He would not, however, agree never to change a line that Shaw had written. Instead, he served time while another Central European, Gabriel Pascal, secured an option from Shaw himself for a five-pound note, which he had borrowed, and a guarantee not to alter a sentence. Within twenty-four hours, Pascal had persuaded Anthony Asquith to direct *Pygmalion* and the Hungarian Leslie Howard to play the lead. He had more persuasive powers than Spiegel himself, and also did not keep his word.

Many of the Central Europeans from the old Hapsburg Empire were doing well in the film business, particularly in Hollywood. There Spiegel decided he would have to return by hook or crook despite his criminal convictions in the United States and in England. "He was guilty of no crimes except those to do with legal tender," John Huston commented. "Sam, as he was wont to do, spent a few days behind bars." He was deported from England back to France, where he wrote the screenplay of a film called *Behind the Facade*, which was shot after he left for Mexico. While in Paris, he heard of the death in Palestine of his father, Simon, who had not completely disowned his black sheep of a younger son. "My father gave me and my brother a good start in life," Spiegel used to joke. "When we cashed it in, I could buy a good dinner."

Spiegel went to Mexico because that was the limbo where the refugees from Europe had to wait before entry to the promised land over the northern border. To pay his fare there, he sold the signed first editions of George Bernard Shaw that Lady Cook had loaned him, but she forgave him for the sake of his need and his charm.

In Mexico City, Spiegel tried to make more films while waiting to arrange matters with the American immigration authorities. A film scripted years later by Billy Wilder showed just how difficult life in Mexico could be. *Hold Back the Dawn*, made in 1941, portrayed Charles Boyer as a Russian playboy trying to marry frumpish Olivia de Havilland in order to achieve entry into the United States: it chronicled some of Wilder's own difficulties in crossing the Rio Grande. Boyer refused to play a scene in which he delivered a soliloquy of despair to a cockroach, but most of the Central Europeans wasting out their years in Mexico had fared no better. Spiegel could claim a daughter resident in the United States, but the overstocked Polish quota of immigrants and his criminal sentences in America and England seemed to exclude him forever.

In 1937, Paul Kohner, who knew Spiegel from Berlin and had achieved his American citizenship, took his wife Lupita Tovar to Mexico City, where she was famous as a film star. On the second night in their new apartment, the telephone rang. It was Spiegel, who had already located them. He told them that he was making two films associated with two other refugees, Jack Gehlmann and Oscar Danziger, while Cantinflas, the great Mexican actor, had agreed to star in them. But what Spiegel wanted was a poker game and a chance to give a party for his star from *The Invader*, Lupita Tovar. The French ambassador would host the party and Spiegel would pay for it. The French ambassador did indeed come to the party, which was held in a restaurant, but Spiegel could not pay for it. In the end, Kohner did, saying, "Sam was still on lean times. He was building his pyramids."

So lean were Spiegel's times that he had to settle his losses at poker games with ancient American five-dollar bills, then out of circulation. His projected films did not get off the ground, but he did manage to sign up a variety show called *Upa Yapa* to be performed at the 1939 World's Fair in New York. It later played under the title of *Mexicana* at the Forty-sixth Street Theater. Spiegel traveled with the show under an assumed name, as he had entered the United States illegally. He claimed that the production was a great artistic success, but earned him no money. "There were one hundred and twenty-six people in the production," he said, "so it won me prestige, but my share of the profits was practically nil, for there were none."

The Mexican government, which had backed the show, did not agree with Spiegel's accounting. He was accused of having absconded with the takings, leaving the dance troupe stranded. On his return to Mexico, he found himself in deep trouble with the authorities. "They were in hot pursuit," the film distributor Max Youngstein remembered, "trying to get him. The Mexican government doesn't like to be fooled with." Spiegel was again sent to jail briefly, John Huston recalled, "but it was always briefly." Rudi Fehr confirmed that Spiegel had sold the Mexican government a bill of goods and had taken a lot of money for himself: after his release from jail, "he walked like a wetback across the border to California." He had no entry papers, he was an illegal immigrant with a Polish passport. But as Paul Kohner said, "Spiegel always wriggled his way from country to country," this time over the border at Laredo in September 1939—the same month that Germany and Russia attacked and partitioned Spiegel's native Poland and began the Second World War.

Spiegel would later return to Mexico in order to go through the process of entering the United States officially, but on this occasion, he reached Hollywood as an illegal alien. Once there, he lived under an assumed name on the charity of other refugee filmmakers from Central Europe. In the American tradition, he would have to invent his life and his reputation all over again. He started in an attic off Sunset Boulevard.

"Not even a picturesque attic," Spiegel said.

CHAPTER FOUR

S. P. Eagle Flies High

If I told you the truth I'd be a hypocrite.
MICHAEL CURTIZ

The second coming of Spiegel to Hollywood was the low period of his life. He had criminal convictions in several countries. He had no past that he would admit. He had no true identity and worked under the false name of S. P. Eagle. He had no American papers and might be deported to any nation that would have him. He had no money in a city which had values mainly calculated in film grosses. All he had was a handful of friends who had known him in Berlin, Vienna and London and a natural charm and energy allied to the desperate skills learned by surviving in an alien world.

There were also class divisions in Hollywood that told against Spiegel. Although many of the chiefs of the film industry came from Eastern Europe, Louis B. Mayer's daughter Irene remembered Spiegel as a joke when he arrived in 1939. His English accent was strange, he lived on Poverty Row. He had not yet achieved that command of the American language that made Lubitsch and Wilder famous. Wilder always used to say his accent was native American compared to Lubitsch's, yet both had a feeling for the local idiom and dialogue. "As Van Gogh said," Wilder joked, "you either have an ear or you don't." The old Hollywood establishment, in Irene Mayer Selznick's opinion, did not go for "all these shoestring Europeans." The newcomers had different standards and were still playing the hustling games that the older Hollywood families had played in their rag-trade days back in New York. It was a case of achieved respectability forgetting how it had been achieved. Yet between the old and the new arrivals "there was a sort of angry and cautious understanding."

What made Spiegel different from the others on Poverty Row were his authority and his apparent learning. He did not yet claim he had a degree from a university. Too many of the other expatriates had spent too much time in Vienna for such claims to pass muster, and Spiegel was not yet enough of an American to reinvent himself daily. He could claim, however, pride in his learned brother, Professor Shalom Spiegel, who had brought over from Palestine his widowed mother, Regina, to stay in America. No leading Hollywood family had so educated a close relation except for Walter Wanger, born in America from distinguished ancestors. To Gottfried Reinhardt, the son of the great theatrical impresario and director Max, Spiegel presented himself as the black sheep of a very good Jewish family, all scholars. "He started from nothing. Motion pictures were not the finest way to make a living. The Germans especially looked down on them." Reinhardt found Spiegel very intelligent and purposeful, bright and talented and competent. Unfortunately, however, his reputation had preceded him. "Spiegel was a congenital crook," Reinhardt commented. "That is proven. He almost preferred to do things deviously. That is the most interesting thing about him, that a man who was so morally despicable was extremely effective in his métier and was to be responsible for some of the best films ever made."

It was the judgment of an established producer from a Viennese theatrical background on a parvenu from Poland who was trying to break into that curious class system that still rules Hollywood, where somebody's status depends on studio connections, past successes, box-office grosses and critical awards. Reinhardt had met Spiegel at the MGM commissary, where Billy Wilder, Walter Reisch, William Wyler and other émigrés were holding a lunchtime domino game. Wilder, Reisch and Wyler were each contributing a hundred dollars a week to keep Spiegel going until he established himself as a producer. It was an additional contribution to the European Film Fund run by Paul Kohner to assist the talented refugees who had fled to Hollywood. Kohner gave a party for Reinhardt to meet Spiegel and join the syndicate to support him. But the two men did not see eye to eye. "I found him not charming at all," Reinhardt recalled. "I thought he looked like a shark." Reinhardt made himself unpopular with his German friends by using the old phrase "Include me out," the phrase Samuel Goldwyn had used when refusing to pay blackmail to the labor racketeer Willie Bioff. It was Reisch and Wilder who secured for Spiegel the rights on a successful prewar German film, *Der Frack*, which itself was derived from another work, the English play *My Lady's Dress*, now adapted to sketches about different people who wear a *man's* evening dress tailcoat. This inspired the screenplay of Spiegel's first Hollywood production, *Tales of Manhattan*, although Lubitsch reckoned that the plots of the film's six episodes were stolen from six different Hungarian playwrights. Spiegel was always at his best bringing together the elements of a production. Eventually ten writers headed by Ben Hecht were to be credited with the screenplay for *Tales of Manhattan*. There was rarely a clear provenance for anything Spiegel did.

Packaging such a film was an incredible idea for a penniless producer, who had no legal right to be in America. He hoped to attract a dozen major Hollywood stars to appear in the six planned episodes. "I didn't have a nickel with which to swing it," Spiegel said later. "I tried every producer in town with the hope of finding some one to back the production, but they all laughed at me." He even tried the Hungarian producer Alexander Korda, temporarily in Hollywood in order to produce films featuring neutral America's involvement on the British side in the war in Europe. But Korda said, "When I am breaking my neck trying to get a single male star for my film *Lydia*, how do you suppose you can get a dozen—and without even a nickel to back you." Ernst Lubitsch actually thought Spiegel was crazy. "He told his secretary after he had talked to me," Spiegel said, "not to let me into his office again, that I was out of my mind."

After a year of getting nowhere, Spiegel approached Boris Morros, then a musical director and producer at Paramount. He became Spiegel's partner and spent the following year helping him to refine the screenplay and to contact possible stars and directors. In September 1941, Morros and Spiegel (under the pseudonym S. P. Eagle) signed a contract with Darryl Zanuck and William Goetz at Twentieth Century–Fox. The two producers received their first check. It was the first regular money that Spiegel had made in two and a half years. "I was mighty glad to see it," Spiegel said in his new American style.

His creditors and backers would also have been mighty glad to see some of it, but they would never see any of their seed money back. As well as his hundred-dollar-a-week contributors from the Central European film world, Spiegel had financed himself during his lean years as an illegal immigrant by questionable means. He was one of the first filmmakers to use illegal gambling money for film production—a common Hollywood practice twenty years later, when laundering skimmed profits from Nevada casinos through celluloid fantasies was to lead to a movie boom. While developing a screenplay with the writer Marcel Achard, Gottfried Reinhardt was spending time in Arrowhead Springs near San Bernardino. The resort hotel was dull, both men were bored. Suddenly Spiegel appeared in the lobby and asked them if they would like to join an illegal game of blackjack, taking place in a cabin in the woods. Achard and Reinhardt lost ten thousand dollars that night, which they did not have on them. Spiegel vouched that their credit was good, they signed markers and were allowed to leave the game unharmed. The next morning they returned to Los Angeles. Later that day, Spiegel appeared in Reinhardt's office to collect the ten thousand dollars. "He was most disagreeable about it," Reinhardt said. "He dunned me for the money. Not only was he a shill, but he was a debt collector. He was always a passionate gambler."

When Spiegel went to New York in October 1941, he met Max Youngstein who was working on marketing for Spyros Skouras and Twentieth Century–Fox. Youngstein's job was to handle "difficult" producers and pictures like John Ford's *How Green Was My Valley*—it was held to be difficult to sell because its subject was striking miners and labor relations. Spiegel and new partner Boris Morros had been engaged as producers in Los Angeles—"two wayward children" hired for the production of *Tales of Manhattan*. Spiegel seemed to Youngstein the perfect imitation of a European trying to be an American. He wore a back-belted camel-hair coat, while the moon-faced, ever-smiling Boris Morros sported a large garnet crucifix outside an Ascot sweater; this shocked Youngstein as all three men were Jewish. Actually, the crucifix was Morros's chief conversation piece, as he claimed that the cross had been given to him when he was conductor of the Moscow Symphony Orchestra by none other than Rasputin. He used to whirl the crucifix on its gold chain like a lasso until he was asked its provenance. He would then reveal in his particular accent, "Razzputin and me, we are the spiritzel-type man."

If Morros failed to impress Youngstein by his connections, Spiegel did impress by his affability and erudition and the motion pictures that he claimed to have made in Germany and in Austria. He had created a great deal of publicity, which had reached the trade papers. Everybody knew of him although did not know exactly why. "It was rather like *Rashomon*," Youngstein recalled. "There were twelve different opinions of everybody— good, bad, indifferent, terrible, trustworthy, Boy Scouts, or what they were." Otto Preminger, who had known Spiegel in Vienna, gave his verdict: "Spiegel is talented, but totally undisciplined. Don't turn your back, because your eyeteeth will be stolen, your hair will be stolen."

European filmmakers in general did have a good reputation in the United States, particularly if they had worked for the great Max Reinhardt. Youngstein found that nobody bothered to check whether or not these two producers were protégés, pupils or acquaintances. "There was just a vogue at the time. Anyone from Europe who was connected with the picture business should be brought over because we would become very intellectualized and we would really be seeing quality as opposed to the schlock we were turning out." Ordered to entertain these cultivated emigrés Spiegel and Morros, Youngstein asked them where they would like to visit in New York. They were expected to say the Statue of Liberty or the Empire State Building or the new Rockefeller Center. But Spiegel insisted on going to Polly Adler's. She ran the best whorehouse in town and hailed from Yanow, a Russian village near the Polish border not too far from Spiegel's birthplace at Jaroslaw. Youngstein could not change Spiegel's mind and was forced to take him there.

It was a civilized place. As Polly Adler wrote, she was concerned with quality and consideration. She called her establishment the equivalent of Bergdorf's and Bonwit's who dressed their windows attractively to pull in trade. She gave her customers personalized service and an attractive house. When Spiegel saw it, he was amazed at its quality and desired it all. "He wanted to have more than one girl, after he had the first girl," Youngstein remembered, "and before you know he wanted all the place. He was like a kid let loose in the proverbial candy store. He was in heaven." He kept Youngstein at Polly Adler's until five in the morning and ran up a bill of more than nine hundred dollars for his five girls and champagne. Youngstein had to sign the expense account and have it countersigned by Bill Michael, the Mussolini of Twentieth Century–Fox in Manhattan. He expected to be fired, but decided to tell the truth. "Mr. Spiegel managed to get me into trouble in the first twenty-four hours I encountered him," he told Michael. The reason why? "Pussy." Michael roared with laughter, signed the expense account and said, "Why didn't you tell me, boy?"

Youngstein believed that only the obscure and charismatic Spiegel could have put together the film of *Tales of Manhattan*. "The cast was the length of your arm and all the best names"— among others, it included Charles Boyer, Rita Hayworth, Ginger Rogers, Henry Fonda, Charles Laughton, Edward G. Robinson, Paul Robeson, Cesar Romero, Elsa Lanchester, James Gleason, and George Sanders. As one reviewer declared, "The film boasts a cast glittering enough to interest everyone but the lads who have to figure out the electric light bulbs on theater marquees." With so many leading stars involved in making a movie, even if they appeared only briefly in one episode out of five, no studio could refuse to back it. In spite of the previous *Grand Hotel*, Paul Kohner credited Spiegel with inventing the packaging deal to create film financing, while his partner Boris Morros secured distribution through Twentieth Century–Fox.

So Spiegel converted a pipe-dream, that he could get most of the major stars to perform for him, into a reality. "He parlayed a pack of lies into a motion picture," the producer John Houseman said. His method was to tell Charles Boyer that Ginger Rogers and Charles Laughton had agreed to appear in the picture, and then tell Ginger Rogers that Boyer and Laughton had signed. By the time Boyer and Rogers had agreed to play on the strength of the acceptances of the other two stars, Laughton easily agreed and admired Spiegel for his technique. He was a practical Yorkshireman and he liked the persistence with which Spiegel got things done. "Spiegel used every method short of getting down on his knees and begging," Max Youngstein remembered, "and I wouldn't put it past Sam to do that. He was one of those remarkable men who had the ability to do something which in somebody else's hands would be crass, gross, and make it look like a class act. He could do that while he was lifting money out of your left pocket and while he was trying to get into your right pocket. You discovered that and forgave him. Somehow or other, there was a combination of the style of what he was trying to do, and great erudition."

Spiegel failed, however, to persuade his friends and private backers, William Wyler or Billy Wilder, to direct *Tales of Manhattan*. Wyler always said that the only way that he could remain friendly with Spiegel was if they did not make a movie together. Billy Wilder felt the same. In the games of dominance played as filmmaking or gin rummy between the Central European refugees, only one could win, and the clashes of personality on the set would have been too great between players of so similar a temperament. In the event, Spiegel never repaid his early backers for their financing of him, except by the generosity of his continuous hospitality. It was not in his nature to be able to bear gratitude to other people who had helped him in lean times. He resembled the proverbial Chinese who had to kill the man who rescued him from drowning because he could not bear the sense of obligation toward somebody who had saved his life. Spiegel had to command, to give, to be the host, to dominate. He never learned how to accept gracefully or how to repay.

He finally selected the expatriate Frenchman Julien Duvivier to direct all the episodes in *Tales of Manhattan*, which bore certain resemblances to Duvivier's past success, *Un Carnet de Bal*. The direction managed, as

Bosley Crowther noted in the *New York Times*, to bring a surprising evenness and delicacy to the various styles of the star actors and to the segments where the tailcoat was passed from back to back. The only pity was that a sixth episode starring the bibulous comic W. C. Fields had to be cut because the final version of the film ran too long. The film opened in 1942 at the Radio City Music Hall and was a critical and a modest financial success.

By this one film, Spiegel made himself a celebrity in Hollywood. Most of the stars and the studio chiefs knew of him. He had a host of friends, contacts and acquaintances. Fortune seemed to have smiled on him, and his film showed taste as well as good judgment. He acquired a house in Beverly Hills at 702 North Crescent Drive on the corner of Carmelina Drive, the wrong side of Sunset Boulevard. There he managed a private club, relaxed and sophisticated, on little apparent money. "He had arrived in Hollywood," John Houseman wrote, "penniless and a fugitive from justice in several countries, including the U.S.A." Yet at his house, "people dropped by after dinner for a drink and stayed on for hours playing backgammon or gin rummy or simply talking." Spiegel was a wizard at gin rummy and won more than enough to pay for the food and the drink that were consumed. The regulars were Billy Wilder and Walter Reisch, the writer Ludwig Bemelmans and the directors John Huston and Willy Wyler (with or without his wife Talli) and Anatole Litvak and Otto Preminger and Ernst Lubitsch. "We all turned to Sam for comfort or shelter," John Huston said, "at one time or another." The gin rummy games involved large losses and temper tantrums. Cards, tables and ashtrays went flying. Enraged at Preminger's taunts one night, Spiegel forgot that he was in his own home and jumped up, shouting, "I'm going. I shall never set foot in this house again."

The games went on. Spiegel had discovered that the secret of success in Hollywood was to become a celebrity and to make contacts with the powerful and to do services for them. Everybody who was anybody wanted to be at Spiegel's *salon* for the company, the drink, the gambling and the girls. "He befriended all the millionaires like Howard Hughes," Rudi Fehr recalled. They had enough money to help Spiegel, they found an attorney to aid him in arranging his immigration problems. The wealthy and the mighty came to Spiegel's residence, which had an element taken from Polly Adler's house that was not a home. "There were always beautiful young things," Fehr said, "showgirls were always there to make some other gentleman happy. I put it delicately."

Spiegel was only following Hollywood's very first social leader, Mack Sennett. "He'd give a dinner party," Walter Wanger remembered, "and if you didn't take the young lady on your right upstairs between the soup and the entrée, you were considered a homosexual." Spiegel had to be more circumspect, but the young girls were always present upstairs. When John Houseman pointed this out in his autobiography, Spiegel threatened to sue him. Houseman telephoned Billy Wilder to check on his memories, only to receive the answer, "Spiegel should have told you he didn't have a second floor."

The atmosphere at Spiegel's house was that of a superior speakeasy where during the years of Prohibition, the respectable world had first mingled with criminals and the worlds of finance, literature, show business and aristocracy. That odd *mélange* of celebrities was created in the twenties, as were the gossip columnists who perpetuated its fame in New York and Los Angeles. Reputations of film people came to be made and broken by the columnists, particularly when the celebrities rebelled against the double standard of the Hollywood studios, so pious and proper under the terms of their production code, so lax and permissive about the private lives of their executives, actors and producers. Anyone could sin as long as he or she was not caught in the act or as long as it could be fixed. But those who were caught and publicized were ruined, as Fatty Arbuckle found out, and Charles Chaplin would.

Spiegel catered to Hollywood's unofficial tastes to make himself a celebrity. He took care not to be found out or named in the newspapers. He was an expert at arranging matters before they became dangerous for him or his friends. "Sam could also be a very good guy," Huston said. "He would break his neck for you. He would go to endless pains for you." He quoted Billy Wilder's observation on Spiegel: "It's the old story, if you woke up in a motel with a dead whore who'd been stabbed, who would you call? D'you know—Sam Spiegel."

Despite producing *Tales of Manhattan*, Spiegel was still an illegal immigrant with a criminal record and no work permit. If the Immigration Department discovered his true identity through the tax authorities, he might be deported to any country that would accept him. He was still not influential enough to settle matters with government institutions. His necessary alias of S. P. Eagle was the subject of a plethora of jokes. Darryl Zanuck suggested that Spiegel next change his name to E. A. Gull, but he himself would not change his name to Z. A. Nuck. Others suggested to Spiegel's director friend Ernst that he change his name to L. U. Bitsch, while Spiegel's next film project should be called *S. T. Ranger*. Spiegel himself gave other reasons for the switch. As the conflict with Hitler's Third Reich loomed, a German name might seem unpatriotic and box-office poison. The British Royal Family itself had become the House of Windsor during the First World War, and the Battenbergs were changed to the Mountbattens. "The attack on Pearl Harbor happened while we were shooting *Tales of Manhattan*," Spiegel later explained, "and I was struck by a burst of patriotism. My German name seemed positively profane in the circumstances, so I renounced it." There were other good local reasons. Most Jews in Hollywood, particularly the actors, made their names sound more Anglo-Saxon; Issur Danielovitch, later Isidore Demsky, altered his name to Kirk Douglas and Judith Tuvim to Judy Holliday, Emmanuel Goldenberg to Edward G. Robinson and David Daniel Kaminsky to Danny Kaye. But Laurence Evans, now a literary agent, heard Spiegel's most extravagant explanation for his metamorphosis to S. P. Eagle. He had consulted the leading Hollywood astrologer and had been told that his fortune would soar only if he took the name of the bird of prey that was the American national symbol.

Spiegel's charm and hospitality and private services overcame the doubts of many of Hollywood's established figures. Talli Wyler viewed him initially with suspicion. "He bore watching," she said, but later became devoted to him. Even when he was poor and legally harassed, she admired his composure and style. "He operated on the edge of a financial precipice better than anybody I ever saw, but the marvelous thing was that somehow he managed to live—or to make you feel he was living—the same way, whether he was either up or down. Living well is the best revenge, and he really did, and he knew how to include his friends in it. I don't know how he did it, but there was always a feeling of lavishness about Sam."

His parties on New Year's Eve became legendary. Few celebrities went to the first two or three of them except for Irene and David Selznick, but by the fourth year, there was nowhere to park and Spiegel was turning uninvited guests away. "There was a sort of flow to them," Walter Reisch's wife, Leisl, said. "Everybody was there, everybody who was anybody and lots of people who were nobody. You could talk to people easily. It was such a show." The staircase led up from the living room, and anybody who sat on the stairs could see everybody entering. "They'd come in just to taste the joint, see what was going on. Sam had a social gift, he knew how to put people together." By the middle of the 1940s, if you were not invited to Spiegel's house on New Year's Eve, you did not rate in Hollywood.

"During World War Two," Sylvia Reinhardt recalled, "he gave the parties. He was generally ingratiating himself." Everyone in Hollywood remembered him for that. Lady Keith, then Mrs. Howard Hawks, found him "always giving a party he couldn't pay for." He had a friendly bank manager, who would loan him two thousand dollars each New Year's Eve to help pay for the occasion: Spiegel had persuaded the bank that his future career in films depended upon the goodwill. He changed his caterers from year to year, because the previous ones were never paid in full. At one New Year's Eve party a guest in the receiving line put a subpoena in Spiegel's hand instead of shaking it. Spiegel read the legal document, shook hands with the server and carried on as if nothing had happened. At another party, a man came to repossess Spiegel's Cadillac. Spiegel waved him away in the car as if he were an honored guest departing. Leaving the Spiegel house late one New Year's Eve, the Columbia Pictures executive Mike Frankovich went to say good-bye to his host. He heard an argument developing in Spiegel's study. Inside was the Beverly Hills chief of police, saying that too many of Spiegel's creditors were complaining and that his furniture would have to be taken away. "After the party," Spiegel said and took five hundred dollars off the chief of police as an investment in his next film production.

"He was most ingratiating," John Huston said. "He exercised his charm with considerable skill. He would borrow a hundred, five hundred, a thousand dollars from a man, then send the man's wife masses of flowers worth half the amount. He wasn't a piker." Spiegel especially charmed women, and more especially beautiful women. To the actress Evelyn Keyes, "Whatever Sam Spiegel was, he conducted himself as if he were beautiful, and you were beautiful." To his neighbor Nadia Gardiner he gave life— he made women feel alive. He created an aura of personal attention and power, like Onassis. He could seduce most women, but not his friends' wives or even Zsa Zsa Gabor, who called his New Year's Eve occasions glorious and beautiful, but insisted that she never had a flirtation with him. "I was always married at his parties."

Spiegel had avoided service in the First World War, and so he did in the Second. He did not believe in fighting other people's battles. "There was nothing cowardly about Sam," in John Huston's opinion, "but he did not court disaster." Huston himself always did, playing—as Orson Welles said—Mephistopheles to his own Faust. But Spiegel did truly care about the fate of the Jews in Europe and the future of a Palestine that refugee Jews might change into an independent Israel. In 1939, one of his screen-writers on *Tales of Manhattan*, Ben Hecht, had decided that he had been turned into a Jew by the German mass murder of his people. Meeting with three organizers of a Jewish secret army, the Irgun Zvai Leumi, and learning about the Jewish Legion, which had fought during the First World War, had made Hecht a supporter and a fund-raiser for an independent Jewish force in Palestine. He was ashamed at the silence of American Jews on the massacres and concentration camps in Europe. They seemed to listen to Joseph Kennedy, the American ambassador in London and former film producer, who claimed that the outcries against the Holocaust would make it appear that a "Jewish war" was being fought against the Fascist powers, not a democratic one.

Turned down by the Hollywood studio bosses, who would help Jews in trouble but not help them make trouble, Hecht organized a mass meeting in 1942 to raise money for his cause. Emotions ran high, people walked out, but one hundred and thirty thousand dollars were pledged by the likes of Spiegel. Unfortunately, after two weeks of grim debt-collecting, only nine thousand dollars were gathered in. Spiegel's pledge of five thousand dollars was never forthcoming. His heart may have been with the resistance in Palestine, but his pockets were empty. "His solvency at that time," Hecht noted in his autobiography, "could be said to be in question."

So was Spiegel's very presence in America. If he had helped in the war effort, he might have received permission to enter the country and work there. As it was, he was discovered under his alias of S. P. Eagle by the immigration authorities. He applied for a pardon against a deportation order, and his case was put before the State Advisory Pardon Board in November 1943. His plea was dismissed and a rehearing was scheduled for December 8 that year. Evidence of his past came out. His conviction and jail sentence in 1929 for passing a bad check had led to his previous deportation to Poland. He had also been arrested in June 1942 in Los Angeles on the charge of cashing several checks without sufficient funds in 1940, although the charge was later dismissed on the ground that Spiegel had made restitution and the complaining witnesses did not wish to prosecute. One month later, he had been fined three hundred dollars for failing to register and be fingerprinted as an alien. These two subsequent offences demonstrated to the lieutenant governor of California, Frederick F. Houser, that Spiegel had failed to rehabilitate himself after his first conviction and parole in 1929. His report to the State Advisory Pardon Board recommended that if Spiegel did not receive a pardon from the governor himself, which he did not, "he will be deported to Mexico as that is the country from which he made his entry to the United States." If Mexico refused to accept him, he would have to be deported, as he had been in 1930, to his native Poland.

That would have meant certain death, as the Nazis now occupied all Poland and were killing off every Jew in the country. Presumably Spiegel would have to have been delivered by parachute from an American bomber. It was the worst time of trial in his life. He could count, however, on the support of the whole of the Jewish community in Hollywood to help him evade his fate. His attorney, Murray Chotiner, had methods of delaying execution of sentence, at least until the fighting in Europe was over and Poland could receive its prodigal son humanely once again. Curiously enough, Spiegel might well have been deported for the second time, never to return to the United States, if the Nazis had not been occupying his homeland. As it was, he lived on in America to fight for his right to stay.

Every once in a while, the immigration officials came too close to Spiegel, and he had to flee over the border to Tijuana to hide out and enter America illegally again. Once his friend the agent Felix Ferry heard that Spiegel was about to be arrested and deported by the Immigration Bureau. He went around to Spiegel's house early in the morning and saw federal officers waiting in a car across the street. Ferry entered by the back door to warn Spiegel, who was asleep. Roused by Ferry, Spiegel telephoned downstairs to order breakfast from his servant.

"The feds are out front," Ferry protested. "You are in big trouble."

"Don't bother me," Spiegel said. "Let me finish my breakfast."

And that is what he did, taking his time. He then had a shower, dressed, put on his usual cologne and instructed his servant to pack a small case and put his car in the back alley. Only then did he leave, while Ferry was shaking in his shoes. It was an admirable display of coolness under pressure worthy of Sir Francis Drake finishing his game of bowls before attacking the Spanish Armada—a quality that Spiegel had developed over decades of learning how to survive. He seemed truly casual. Yet, as Evelyn Keyes noticed, one had the impression he felt he was on borrowed time.

After four more years of legal battles and gaining influential friends, Spiegel secured an incredible reversal of law and fortune. Hiring as his attorney Edward J. O'Connor, the nephew of federal judge J. F. T. O'Connor, Spiegel had his deportation order eased so that he could leave the United States voluntarily. He then entered a belated plea of not guilty to the charge of passing a bad check on which he had been convicted in 1929. The plea was permitted to stand, although Spiegel had originally pleaded guilty and had served time; these facts were expunged from the record in his immigration dossier. After this unprecedented act of oblivion in spite of the true facts, attorney O'Connor obtained a series of delays on the execution of the deportation order. Spiegel also discovered something which he had forgotten, that he had applied for a permit to enter the United States from Poland in 1930 immediately after his previous deportation there. He was thus high on the quota for admission as a Polish immigrant.

His daughter Alisa, now herself an American citizen, applied for her father's admission under a preferential status in the quota. She did this even though she had not seen her father between her babyhood in Palestine and her sixteenth birthday, when he had already completed the production of *Tales of Manhattan*. And on September 12, 1947, Spiegel went to Tijuana, on a flying visit with his attorney O'Connor so that he could cross the Mexican border into the United States under the provisions of the Polish quota, where his number had come up. Because of his daughter's application and the deletion of his criminal record, Spiegel's request for admission to the United States was accepted favorably and permission was given him to apply for citizenship. After nineteen years, Spiegel was welcome in America.

CHAPTER FIVE

Hollywood Years

She might do worse marrying him.
But for the life of me I can't think how.

ROBERT MORLEY

In 1948, at a party in the little English garden of Lewis Milestone's house, the knowledgeable writer and producer Eddie Chodorov was approached by a young blonde of extraordinary beauty, under the Chinese lanterns hanging from the trees. She needed his private advice. Her name was Lynn Baggett, and Warner Brothers wanted to renew her acting contract. Sam Spiegel wanted to marry her. And her mother wanted her to return to Texas and settle down. What should she do?

"Miss Baggett," Chodorov said, "off the cuff, gut reaction—I don't see any signs of you becoming a star. So far as marrying Sam Spiegel, you ask me—and that is your answer. If you wanted to, I couldn't hold you back. If you marry him, you will be put in the company of very tough, difficult men. I don't know how many girls have jumped off the Hollywood sign because of these men—they are not evil, but tough, and I find it difficult to cope with them on my own."

Chodorov told Lynn Baggett that she was an innocent. If he were her, he would take her mother's advice: go back to Texas, marry an oil million-aire and have children. He then left the party at the Milestones', and went home. At 3.30 A.M., Spiegel was on the telephone, asking him what weapons he wanted to use.

"What for?" Chodorov asked.

"We are going to have a duel. You told Lynn not to marry me."

Briefly wondering if Spiegel were not confusing himself with Erich von Stroheim, Chodorov parried the charge.

"I did in a way tell her not to marry you. I told her, in my opinion, it would be a mistake. I think you will end with that opinion yourself."

"Revolvers?" Spiegel asked.

"It's a Greek tragedy," Chodorov said. "Go ahead and do it. Leave me out. She was indiscreet to tell you. She's that unsuitable."

Chodorov heard no more from Spiegel, who did go ahead and marry the beautiful and romantic actress of twenty-one, less than half his age. She was an American citizen and, as in Billy Wilder's script *Hold Back the Dawn*, the marriage confirmed Spiegel's own American citizenship. The news of the wedding of S. P. Eagle to a starlet, Wilder now said, "left Hollywood S. P. Eechless." John Huston, then married to Evelyn Keyes, flew to Las Vegas for the wedding, but began gambling and never got to the ceremony.

Lynn was always late for everything. She would not go to bed and would haunt the late-night movie shows and clubs, then sleep all day. She wanted no responsibility; there was no solidarity in the marriage. Spiegel and she quickly reached a mutual arrangement that they would live their separate lives, yet she would be his hostess at the house. He taught her one trick at the huge parties, where the champagne and the hot dogs for seven hundred were supplemented by caviar. He stationed her by the huge silver bowl of sturgeon's eggs with a small ladle. "Don't let people just slob it on by themselves," he instructed her. "You do it, and put just a little bit on." Sometimes she appeared at the parties naked under a mink coat for effect, saying that her husband did not give her money to buy clothes.

Spiegel liked to control his wives, his parties, his film productions and his friends' lives. He had to have people about him all the time or on call. If a friend or a mistress went away, he had to have a telephone number to remain in touch. He wanted always to know what all his friends were doing or making. "He liked to be on top of things," Talli Wyler asserted. "Always in control." Yet his talent for persuading people to do what he wanted to do or to invest in him became part of the Hollywood vocabulary. To be "spiegeled" meant to be soothed, cajoled or conned.

These were the contacts, the methods and the qualities that Spiegel brought to his next productions in Hollywood. After completing *Tales of Manhattan*, Spiegel had prepared other projects to produce with Boris Morros: a follow-up based on the English novel *The White Evening Gown*, and a musical featuring the tunes of Rimsky-Korsakov and a chorus of Russian marines. Making no headway on these projects Spiegel looked for other partners and opportunities. He could not write or direct himself, but he liked to use the genius of others, even if they were out of fashion, especially when they were out of employment and cost him little. He bought a story in 1945 from Victor Trivas about a Nazi war criminal who escaped to South America and then turned up as a teacher in a small town in Connecticut, determined to revive Fascist values although Hitler had been defeated. Spiegel paid Tony Veiller and his friend John Huston to write a screenplay. It was the time when the first draft of a screenplay was usually written by "a construction man" from Central Europe, whatever his command of English. The construction man was meant to outline the film. "Middle Europeans were highly regarded for this job," Elia Kazan remembered. "Their knowledge of our language and country was slight but they were hell on structure and continuity." Afterwards, a "dialogue man" was brought in, followed by a "polish man." In the case of *The Stranger*, John Huston was responsible for both the final dialogue and the polish. He was meant to direct the film as well; but Spiegel wanted Orson Welles to play the part of the criminal, and he feared that Welles would not accept the role unless he was allowed to direct.

Huston went off to make a film based on the B. Traven book, *The Treasure of the Sierra Madre*, while Spiegel persuaded Welles to direct and act in his film under terms that Welles had always refused to accept before. Only William Goetz, head of the small International Pictures, would trust Welles to make a motion picture after his box-office failures with *Citizen Kane* and *The Magnificent Ambersons* and the cancelation during shooting of *It's All True*. Welles had to agree to pay back the financing, if he did not complete the picture on its small budget. He also had to agree to give artistic control to the studio and to his producer, "S. P. Eagle." He even had to submit the script for cutting by his assigned editor, Ernest Nims, so that no unnecessary sequences would be shot. The final storyline was lean, straightforward and necessary, with none of the ambiguities that usually made Welles's films so rich and rare. He called Nims and Spiegel his nemesis.

The Stranger was shot at the Goldwyn studios in six weeks, under schedule and under budget. Welles's only extravagance was to engage his art director from *Citizen Kane* to build a tall clock-tower, in which grotesque Germanic figures revolved round the clockface—an unlikely expressionist touch for Connecticut. Spiegel insisted that an unenthusiastic Edward G. Robinson would play the war crimes commissioner who tracked down the Nazi criminal. The star's only comment was that Welles seemed to have run out of genius while making the film, "It was bloodless, and so was I." The truth was that Welles could not stomach the restrictions that he had accepted. His freedom of action was limited, and his genius was put in a straitjacket. His equilibrium was not improved during the filming by being thrown out of his house by his wife, Rita Hayworth, for his infidelities and having to move down Carmelina Drive to Spiegel's house on the corner of Crescent. He was also being falsely accused of an attempted rape, a blackmail that he had to pay off to avoid a prosecution and a scandal. Like Spiegel in Hollywood, he had to appear respectable because of the demands of the studio system.

The Stranger was neither a critical nor a commercial success. It was released by RKO Pictures and failed. Bosley Crowther echoed Edward G. Robinson in calling it a bloodless, manufactured show, a custom-made melodrama that became a routine and mechanical cat-and-rat chase. The atom-bomb newsreels on the same bill were immeasurably more frightening.

Ernst Lubitsch died of a heart attack in December 1947. Above all, his films had brought a wit and a style from Central Europe to the American cinema, and had made many of the German and Austrian émigrés acceptable in Hollywood. He was tremendously amused by Spiegel, telling his writer friend Mary Anita Loos that he was always wide-eyed at Spiegel's perfidy, particularly in stealing all six plots in *Tales of Manhattan* from different Hungarian playwrights who were all bound to sue after the Second World War was over. "But typically, Sam Spiegelwise, he was not in trouble, somehow or other, it just got forgotten."

Lubitsch was also amazed at the prodigal Spiegel hospitality, although nobody ever seemed to get paid for providing it. The caterers appeared to work for nothing because of the privilege of serving "the jampack of everybody in town." Spiegel endeared himself to old European expatriates by his charm and indestructability. "He was the Thief of Baghdad," Mary Anita Loos remembered him, "but right out in the open. But socially and in a friendly way, everybody loved him. Lubitsch loved him. All of the old boys from the past loved him."

He could not, however, continue to live on nothing. Looking round for another project and another partner in 1948, Spiegel ran into John Huston again at the actress and sculptor Salka Viertel's house. He was hardly ever asked there, because of her disapproval of his rival *salon* with its facilities for male guests. Mrs. Viertel was close to Greta Garbo, who had asked her, "Why don't you write?" She began to write most of Garbo's later screenplays, most notably the historical *Queen Christina* and *Conquest* and *Anna Karenina*. Soon separated from her husband, she began an affair with Gottfried Reinhardt that lasted for a decade. Her home in Mabery Road in Santa Monica was a magnet for distinguished refugees—the writers Heinrich and Thomas Mann, Bruno Frank and Bertolt Brecht, the composers Arnold Schoenberg and Igor Stravinsky, and most of the film directors from Berlin. Sam Spiegel was *non persona grata*. The social divisions among the German-speaking immigrants to California were as acute as they had been in the Hapsburg Empire. The way from Mabery Road to Crescent Drive was as long as from Vienna to Galicia. And Salka Viertel's home was a family home, not a wayside house or a rendezvous. Much of Gottfried Reinhardt's disapproval of Spiegel was the attitude of those, who wished to seem as respectable as Hollywood wished to seem, and so had to condemn those who behaved as Hollywood actually did.

Yet on this rare visit to his rival establishment, Spiegel discovered that John Huston had run across *Rough Sketch*, a story in a book written by a New York journalist dealing with the corrupt and reactionary regime in Cuba and a revolutionary attempt to upset it. He worked on a screenplay with Salka's son, the writer Peter Viertel, that prophesied a later Cuban revolution. Huston had met the young John Garfield and wanted him to play the lead. As Garfield was already being persecuted by the House Un-American Activities Committee for his Communist associations, he found it difficult to get work and readily agreed to play the part. Spiegel said that he would produce the picture if Huston formed a company with him. Over the years in London and Hollywood, Huston had learned to recognize Spiegel's good judgment and imagination. He formed Horizon Pictures in partnership with Spiegel, although they usually referred to it as Shit Creek Productions. It was one of the first director-producer associations, independent of the studio system, which was beginning to break up.

Spiegel wanted to take the Cuban project to Louis B. Mayer at MGM, but the night before the meeting was scheduled, Huston got riotously drunk at Humphrey Bogart's anniversary party, which ended with football being played in the living room. Unable to drive home, he stayed at Bogart's place and was woken, suffering from a hangover, by Spiegel on the telephone. Huston had to come to the meeting with Louis B. Mayer. Spiegel dressed Huston in one of his own sports jackets, over Huston's evening dress trousers and patent leather shoes, although the cuffs hardly reached below Huston's elbows. At the MGM meeting, Huston was unable to say a word, while Spiegel rose and described the story of the Cuban film. It was one of the finest demonstrations of pure animal courage that Huston had ever witnessed. Spiegel made the plot up as he went along, but it seemed to make sense. Mayer and his board said that they would consider the proposal and eventually approved the project, but Huston heard that they were dubious about Spiegel, whom they thought something of a rogue and unfit to become a member of their snobbish club. Huston, on the other hand, was approved as a gentleman—for his inarticulateness and his dress—and was offered a two-picture contract.

Spiegel, however, took the Cuban project to the rough Harry Cohn at Columbia Pictures and was offered a better deal on condition that the film was called *We Were Strangers*. Cohn liked Spiegel for his talent and ignored his past reputation. But the necessary casting of Hollywood stars created a problem. John Garfield and Jennifer Jones were not Cubans. "Nothing I or God Almighty could have done," Huston said, "could have made them so." There was an air of falsehood about the film that was not in the writing or in the locations. Most of it was filmed in Cuba, where Huston became quite good friends with Ernest Hemingway, who talked a great deal about death and the changing colors of unburied bodies. In a graveyard sequence, Huston played one of the practical jokes that had given him the title of "The Monster" in Hollywood. While Jennifer Jones was digging among fresh graves in a real cemetery, she unearthed a human hand and screamed blue murder. It was a prop, planted by Huston, to surprise her.

The interiors of *We Were Strangers* were shot in the Columbia Pictures studio: Huston went over schedule and over the budget of nine hundred thousand dollars. Spiegel was unhappy with the ending, in which the hero and the police chief died and the revolution unexpectedly succeeded. He asked Billy Wilder to write an alternative ironic conclusion, which Huston turned down as it did not fit his concept. When Wilder asked why he had been brought in at all, Spiegel riposted, "What makes you think you can write an ending to a John Huston picture?"

Spiegel never appeared to be in the wrong. He needed to dominate and, as Fred Zinnemann pointed out, "being a producer was the apt platform for that kind of psychology." Spiegel had already vetted Zinnemann as a possible director in 1945, giving him lunch at Lucey's, a fashionable circular stucco restaurant on Melrose that looked like a gasoline storage tank. Zinnemann felt that he was being assessed like a horse or a greyhound facing a breeder. He did not pass the test, telling Spiegel openly that he had been replaced by Vincente Minnelli on his last film because he could not get on with Judy Garland. Spiegel found Zinnemann far too honest to employ: it was not his style.

Yet he was a very efficient producer. His secretary, Gladys Hill, ran all the details of his life—or those, in John Huston's opinion, which bore scrutiny. "She was part and parcel of everything Sam did. She defended him in the most discreet way, and protected him. Her façade Sam operated behind. She wasn't in collusion with Sam, for she was an individual with the highest ethics so far as she herself was concerned." Later, after a broken marriage, she was to work for Huston himself for decades, but in the 1940s she was the necessary respectable cover on Spiegel's life.

Yet he himself did the deals and the worrying over money, contracts, time, schedules, stars and distribution. Although he rarely appeared on set and usually allowed the director to have his way there, he interfered in the writing of the drafts of the screenplay and in the editing of the film. Music was one of his particular concerns. He had a definite ear for it. He enjoyed confrontations and provoking artists and technicians to do better. "He had to have a bone to gnaw," Lady Keith noticed, "to make a creative mechanism function, even if making a movie is a very dumb process."

During the shooting of *We Were Strangers* at Columbia Studio, Huston met Marilyn Monroe. It was the beginning of her film career. "She was a lovely little thing, absolutely lovely," Huston said. "She used to come to the set and watch the shooting. She knew Sam Spiegel." Huston's wife, Evelyn Keyes, had often met her at Spiegel's home on Crescent Drive, where she was one of his regular house girls, available for those of his friends who pleased her. There Evelyn Keyes had seen only "one more little blonde with the preferred size tits and a funny walk." Yet when she later was to act with Monroe in *The Seven Year Itch*, directed by Billy Wilder, she saw Monroe with different eyes. "Success had given her a nice patina, a certain glow."

Marilyn Monroe's lover at this time was her agent Johnny Hyde, and she would sit at the back of the room reading a novel while he played gin rummy with Spiegel and Billy Wilder. Huston felt that Marilyn Monroe was being set up for the casting couch rather than the studio floor and offered to give her a screen test with John Garfield. Spiegel said that Horizon Pictures could not afford the test, and it was canceled. Marilyn Monroe disappeared off the set, but in his next film, *The Asphalt Jungle*, Huston did give Monroe her test and the part of the gangster's moll Angela. She was always grateful to Huston for launching her and for saving her from the eternal casting couch. Later Billy Wilder was to make his second film with Monroe, the comedy *Some Like It Hot*. "Breasts of granite," he said after her performance, "and a mind like a Gruyère cheese." But he also said of her press and her misfortunes that she was Hollywood's Joan of Arc, and that he had never seen anyone so fabulous on screen, not even Greta Garbo.

Huston was getting into political trouble along with John Garfield. This compromised the financing of Horizon Pictures, because Louis B. Mayer and the other studio chiefs were as patriotic and anti-Communist as only immigrants from Russia and Poland could be. The progressive politician Henry Wallace was running for President in 1948 against Tom Dewey and Harry Truman, and was being backed by liberals and radicals and a few Communist organizations. Huston agreed to help to organize a Wallace for President Committee in Hollywood. Spiegel was furious. He believed that the reactionary Harry Cohn at Columbia would stop the financing on *We Were Strangers*, which was already over budget. He was thought to be in difficulties over money, and Hollywood was no place to be thought to be in difficulties over anything. The situation was made worse by Huston telling Peter Viertel of Spiegel's trial at the Old Bailey in London, so that Viertel would answer questions about whether Spiegel had financial problems, "Not really. At this stage of production, Sam is usually in jail."

We Were Strangers was completed in 1949 and failed on every count. Politically it was a disaster, especially as the House Un-American Activities Committee was conducting its hearings designed to detect Red influences on the air and the screen. While the Communist *Daily Worker* called the film capitalist propaganda, the *Hollywood Reporter* called it a shameful handbook of Marxist dialectics and the heaviest dish of Red theory ever served to an audience outside the Soviet Union. To the *New York Times*, it was a morbid melodrama, a passionless action film. Harry Cohn hated it, and Columbia Pictures killed its release, so that it was a financial Armageddon. This did not please Spiegel, who protested that he was a dyed-in-the-wool capitalist who resented people saying his latest picture was communistic. "I still like to make a legitimate profit," he said. "Anyone who criticizes the picture on the basis that it supports tyrants is in favor of tyrants." Was not the United States of America born in a fight against the tyranny of King George the Third? Why not look with favor on a revolt against a bloodier tyrant in Cuba? His pleas fell on deaf ears, and compromised his two future productions, Frank Harris's "Reminiscences of a Cowboy" and *The Third Secret*, a script written by Hecht and Huston based on Dostoevsky's "The Eternal Husband," and intended to star James

Mason with Lewis Milestone as the director.

Spiegel himself was being threatened by the hearings of the House Un-American Activities Committee, which appealed to those grassroots Americans who disliked foreigners, Jews, Reds and subversives. It was no accident that ten of the nineteen Hollywood people subpoenaed by the committee were Jewish, and that there were six Jews among the Hollywood Ten who were finally indicted. And disaster finally struck Horizon Pictures itself when the actor Sterling Hayden decided to name some names to the committee. One of them was Bea Winters, a woman who had been his mistress and had recruited him for the Communist party. She was presently working at Horizon for Spiegel. As reported in the *New York Times*, Bea Winters was "instructed not to come back to work until she had cleared herself. Her immediate superior, Gladys Hill, acting on advice from the company's attorney, declared that Miss Winters would be fired if it should be established that she *is* a Communist." She was soon fired, and the unhappy Sterling Hayden, as he described himself in his memoir, *Wanderer*, swung like a goon from role to role in his new status as a sanitary culture hero.

Hayden also noticed that some producers knew very well how to buy cheaply under the table the work of those on the blacklist. Spiegel was one who was ready to exploit the situation. One hundred and fifty-one talented Hollywood writers and directors and actors were named by a smear-sheet, *Red Channels*, as associates of Communist fronts. Those who were named found it difficult or impossible to get work in Hollywood for the next ten years. Spiegel employed some of them as he had employed Orson Welles, because they were the best at their craft, were available and cost less than they were worth. In Irene Mayer Selznick's opinion, he used politics to his advantage, paying the blacklisted people less than he should. But he did pay them. From their ranks, he took three screenwriters and one director, risking his connections with the Hollywood studios. "Spiegel was clever enough not to be caught in anything," Mike Frankovich from Columbia Pictures said. "But he never ran away from anything. He could have been accused of things."

From those in trouble, Dalton Trumbo and Carl Foreman and Michael Wilson were to work for Spiegel, as well as Joseph Losey in one of his last Hollywood films before he felt obliged to leave for Europe. Losey had failed the litmus test for loyalty: he had refused to direct *I Married A Communist*, later made as *The Woman on Pier 13*. John Huston was nearly denounced as a Communist by the studio chief Jack Warner who accused Howard Koch because of the screenplay of the Woodrow Wilson film, *In Our Time*. Huston was no Communist sympathizer, but he had also been a screenwriter on *In Our Time*; his good fortune was that Jack Warner forgot to name him. Not that Warner's testimony was worth much, as he also stated to the House Un-American Activities Committee that he had never seen a Communist and would not know one if he saw one.

Huston joined with William Wyler and the screenwriter Philip Dunne in forming the Committee for the First Amendment to defend the Hollywood Ten, who had been sentenced to jail for refusing to answer questions about their Communist affiliations. Katharine Hepburn, Gregory Peck, the Bogarts, Kirk Douglas, Gene Kelly, Edward G. Robinson, Burt Lancaster, Billy Wilder and many others joined the committee and flew to Washington to complain to their Californian congressman about the witch-hunt and do what good they could. Spiegel did not go with the committee members to Washington. As a recently naturalized American citizen and as a producer who had to deal with the reactionary studio bosses, he felt too vulnerable to take a political stance. Privately, he helped the victims of persecution, but he did not parade his feelings. "The very fact that he was a foreigner," Max Youngstein said, "made him feel that he was going to be more suspect than a man born in Des Moines with the American flag sticking out of both ears."

At some risk to himself, Spiegel did arrange for one of the Hollywood Ten, Dalton Trumbo, to work on the screenplay of his next film, *The Prowler*, which was credited only to Hugo Butler. Trumbo actually recorded the voice of the cuckolded husband in the film and got thirty-five dollars for his "dubious vocal talents." It took him five years and a lawsuit against Spiegel to receive the last payment due on the $7,500 owed on the script. The director, Joseph Losey, complained that Trumbo wrote in the camera angles, but Trumbo replied that both of them were handicapped craftsmen—a director who couldn't write and a writer who couldn't direct—but as crippled professionals they were as hopelessly dependent on each other as a team of one-legged acrobats.

Spiegel himself had a good experience with the difficult Losey and had few battles with him. *The Prowler* was a veiled answer to the House Un-American Activities Committee; it was full of a sense of danger and threat to liberty under the guise of a *film noir* about a murderous policeman and an unfaithful wife. The representative of the law destroyed all civilized values and was gunned down in a ghost town in the desert. Van Heflin played the cop and Huston's wife, Evelyn Keyes, the distracted mistress. Keyes herself was in a similar situation with her husband, who had begun an affair with his next wife, then a girl of eighteen. At a new restaurant with Spiegel, Keyes hauled a straying blonde off Huston's lap by the hair and shouted, "Listen, you, I'm his wife, and that's his mistress over there, and you are one too many."

Spiegel provided Losey with the best technicians possible for *The Prowler*, including the Oscar-winning cameraman Arthur Miller, who gave what was to be his last film a clarity and a hard edge fitting the lean, honest dialogue. At one moment, Heflin asked Keyes about her failed career as an actress. "Didn't you have enough pull?" He received only the answer, "I was just a little short of talent." The film was not. It engaged all the talents and was made on a small budget with incredible speed and efficiency. Losey had the principal set built down to the last detail. He rehearsed his actors and technicians for only fifteen days, then shot the whole film in nineteen days. He followed John Huston's advice: "Never forget that the screen has three dimensions." The film achieved a depth behind its apparent simplicity. It bore Losey's signature more than it did Spiegel's, who was still searching for his personal stamp on a picture.

Losey said that he was proud of the film, as it was about a hundred thousand dollars, a Cadillac and a blonde, "the *ne plus ultra* of American life at that epoch." His opinion of his producer was that Spiegel was heavily in debt and not doing well, but extremely cultivated, intelligent and sensitive. Spiegel was, however, a megalomaniac. Losey had to refuse to see the rushes of the previous day's takes with Spiegel because he was told how to reshoot them, and he had to throw Spiegel off the set, when the producer tried to intervene. "I became uncontrollable with rage sometimes with Spiegel. But generally he was a good producer for me at that time."

The Prowler was well made and a modest success with the critics and at the box office. United Artists, which released the picture, was encouraged to continue their association with Spiegel. It compensated them for a shoestring production by Spiegel that hardly achieved release at all. *When I Grow Up* was written and directed by Michael Kanin; it was the story of a problem child, played by Bobby Driscoll—he learned from the experiences of his old grandfather, a member of the famous American circus family, the Hannefords. They spent their time, in Huston's words, "jumping on and off the backs of white horses." Even though he was

Kinematograph WEEKLY

No. 1509   Thursday, March 19, 1936   Vol. 229

C. M. Woolf Group Tie-up With Universal

FINANCE FOR BIG AMERCAN DEAL

STATEMENT SHORTLY

THE purchase of Carl Laemmle's interest in Universal Pictures Corporation, which became effective by the deposit this week of a cheque for a million and a half dollars by Standard Capital Corporation, will have important results in this country as well as in America.

As is well known, Charles M. Woolf, managing director of General Film Distributors and British and Dominions Film Corporation, is interested in the deal, and the King cable from New York states definitely that General Film Distributors will distribute Universal product in the United Kingdom.

Films made by General Film Distributors affiliated companies will be available for marketing in America by Universal, who will make a selection of the most suitable product.

The financial interest held by C. M. Woolf interests in the new deal is reported to be two million dollars.

Standard Capital Corporation will deposit securities with Universal to cover the balance of the deal within 61 days from Friday last.

Under the new arrangement R. H. Cochrane, who has been vice-president for many years, becomes president of Universal, with Charles Rogers vice-president.

The English part of the deal was contingent upon the success of Standard Capital to buy the Laemmle interests; now that this is being achieved Mr. Woolf's earlier negotiations become fully operative.

It is generally believed that the deal will result in an exchange of stars and other evidences of close working between the British and the American units.

At the moment of going to press Mr. Woolf was not ready to issue a statement regarding the deal, but this is expected shortly.

C. M. WOOLF

BRITISH COLOUR FACTORY TO COST £250,000

TECHNICOLOR LABORATORY ENLARGED

Technicolor, Ltd., the £250,000 capital of which has been recently increased by £50,000, has acquired a site of 11 acres on the Great West Road at Harmondsworth.

A laboratory is now in the course of construction, and will cost, when fully equipped, about £250,000. The plant will have a capacity of 80 ft. per minute of four-colour Technicolor prints.

Technicolor, Ltd. will commence their first British production in May for London Film Productions, Ltd., and also for New World Productions, Ltd.

The Council commended as "a good standard of architecture" the elevations and drawings of the proposed buildings which were submitted by Technicolor when they applied for the zoning of the land at Batheaud for the factory.

It is announced that six companies have signed with Technicolor in this country, and Kay Harrison, the managing director, states that it has been decided to double the capacity of the studio now being erected.

SAM SPIEGEL REMANDED

Samuel Spiegel (M), Polish citizen and company director, of Great Cumberland Place, Marble Arch, when he appeared on remand at Marylebone Police Court on Tuesday, March 17, was also charged with forging a guarantee to the prejudice of Edmund J. Cubbardson ("Teddy") Joyeel.

Evidence having been given, the accused was remanded on bail of two sureties of £500 each.

FILMS CUT UNDER ADVERTISED LENGTH

Bristol C.E.A. Members' Complaint

MEMBERS of the Bristol and West of England C.E.A. branch met on Tuesday, under the chairmanship of A. B. Atkinson.

Discussion arose on the difficulty that confronted an exhibitor when a film which he had booked on the understanding that it was a certain length, proved to be considerably shorter when it was received for showing.

Another complaint concerned the old grievance that still pictures sent as advance publicity frequently illustrated scenes which did not appear in the film itself.

These points had already been raised at other branch meetings, and necessary action is to be taken through the usual offices of the Association.

A member reported that he had had an application for admission at reduced prices for the Railway Queen.

The Chairman pointed out that a resolution was on the books of the branch against making any differentiation in prices of admission for any particular class of public.

TOP Buster Keaton pricks a legend in *The Invader*, 1935

LEFT 'Sam Spiegel Remanded', March 1936

ABOVE Ginger Rogers and Henry Fonda in *Tales of Manhattan*, 1942

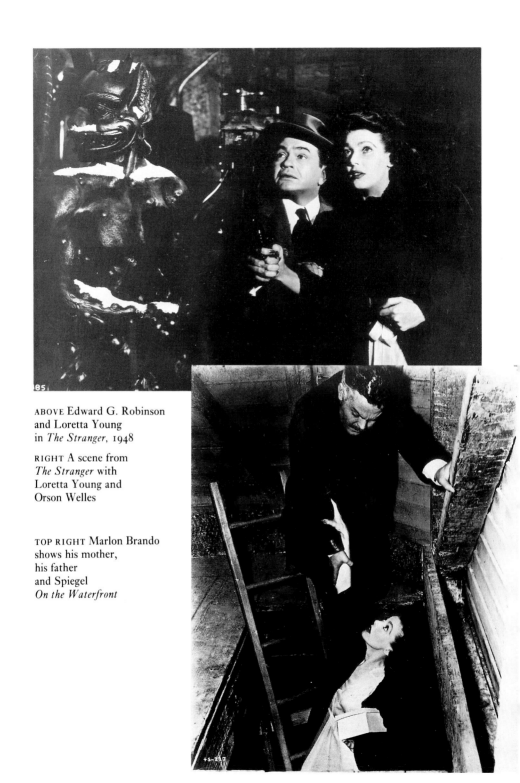

ABOVE Edward G. Robinson
and Loretta Young
in *The Stranger*, 1948

RIGHT A scene from
The Stranger with
Loretta Young and
Orson Welles

TOP RIGHT Marlon Brando
shows his mother,
his father
and Spiegel
On the Waterfront

ABOVE The *African Queen* tows Humphrey Bogart, Katharine Hepburn and the crew up the Congo

LEFT Bogart and Hepburn tow the *African Queen* through the English marshes

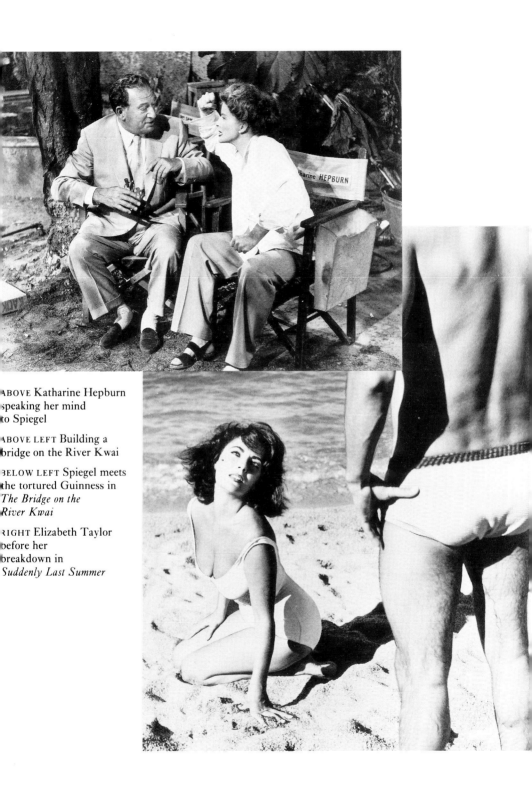

ABOVE Katharine Hepburn
speaking her mind
to Spiegel

ABOVE LEFT Building a
bridge on the River Kwai

BELOW LEFT Spiegel meets
the tortured Guinness in
*The Bridge on the
River Kwai*

RIGHT Elizabeth Taylor
before her
breakdown in
Suddenly Last Summer

Peter O'Toole in *Lawrence of Arabia*

ABOVE LEFT Gary Cooper gives Spiegel his Oscar

ABOVE CENTRE Spiegel tells Marlon Brando what to do about *The Chase*

LEFT David Lean and Spiegel confront each other

With Anthony Quinn and Elliot Silverstein on location for *The Happening*
TOP Henri-Georges Clouzot, Romy Schneider and Spiegel aboard the *Malahne,* 1963
ABOVE RIGHT Omar Sharif and Peter O'Toole in *Night of the Generals*
BELOW RIGHT Spiegel at the Finland Station in *Nicholas and Alexandra*

Adam with his mother,
Ann Pennington

RIGHT Adam Spiegel,
aged sixteen, in a play
at Westminster School

LEFT ABOVE Ann Pennington,
Kirk Douglas and Spiegel
aboard the *Malahne*

CENTRE ABOVE On holiday
with his son Adam

LEFT Father and son

Harold Pinter
listening to
Spiegel

RIGHT Ingrid Boulting
and Spiegel
on the set of
The Last Tycoon

Spiegel's partner in Horizon Pictures, Huston had nothing to do with this film, although he did put his signature on dozens of papers that Gladys Hill brought for him to sign, until he was advised not to do so. Spiegel was living off his producer's expenses while performing the juggling acts needed to scrape together the financing for *The Prowler* and *When I Grow Up*. However the movies did, Spiegel survived.

Although he had no money, the entertaining and the illusion of success were maintained. George Stevens, Jr., who later made *Shane* and *Giant*, was called in by Spiegel to talk about directing a film. He said that he had his doubts about Spiegel's financial stability. Spiegel protested that he had more than enough money to make the picture. At that moment, there was a thunderous knocking on Spiegel's door. Spiegel refused to move or make a sound. It was probably the sheriff's office. Eventually, the intruders went away, and Spiegel continued to say that he had his full budget for the proposed film, but George Stevens refused to direct for him. "It didn't give me the greatest sense of confidence at that time."

At a dinner at Romanoff's to celebrate the wrap of *When I Grow Up*, the journalist Erskine Johnson saw reason for Spiegel to celebrate. "Completing films was his problem in those days. But this was one he did complete." Joined by other celebrities, they had a fine dinner at Romanoff's which allowed Spiegel more credit for fear that he would never pay his existing debts to the restaurant. Spiegel signed the expensive bill, then buttonholed Cary Grant and Tyrone Power on the sidewalk outside. "Have you got a couple of bucks?" he asked. "I need the cab fare home."

The famous New Year's Eve parties at Spiegel's house on Crescent Drive went on until the end of the 1940s. Sidney (later Lord) Bernstein found Spiegel himself a man of impeccable taste, but his parties full of vulgar people, all of whom Bernstein would have thrown out. But this was hardly the opinion of anyone else in the film world, particularly not of Radie Harris of the *Hollywood Reporter*. In her reminiscences, she quoted Truman Capote's dictum that there were only two parties to give: for six or four hundred. Spiegel gave them for five hundred, and if you were not one of the five hundred "most intimate friends invited, you were a social leper and you might just as well have worn a Scarlet Letter when you were seen in public."

By 1950, however, even Spiegel had enough of his New Year's Eve gatherings. The aftermath was not worth the publicity or the cost. "We couldn't live in the place for a week afterwards," he said. "Even after the litter was all cleared up, you couldn't get the smell of cigarette smoke or liquor fumes off the walls." He felt that he was aging, and so he held his final New Year's Eve party at Lucey's Restaurant, where more than a thousand people were invited. By Spiegel's own admission, it was a shambles, with standing room only in something approaching the Black Hole of Calcutta. He also called it the wrap party for *The Prowler* and persuaded John Huston, Evelyn Keyes, and Van Heflin each to put up "a quarter" of its cost of $3,200, leaving him with only $800 to pay himself. There was fury at Horizon Films later when it was discovered that the full cost of the party had been put on the budget while Spiegel pocketed the difference.

But the Hollywood years were coming to an end. Spiegel had not yet achieved a success in financial terms with any film. He lived on the margins and on his wits, even if he was known all about town. But he was soon to be called back to Europe. He had his American citizenship and his American passport, so he could now leave the United States. His next film for United Artists would bring him fame and fortune. It would be made in Africa and England, that country which had deported him before the Second World War.

CHAPTER SIX

The African Queen

But it was an awfully clever piece of direction, wasn't it? Very bright.
KATHARINE HEPBURN

News of the persecution by a congressional committee of many of the more talented filmmakers in Hollywood reached London. Two young producers, John and Jimmy Woolf, whose father was a major British film distributor, had decided that Anglo-American film productions were the wave of the future. Their first deal was with Albert Lewin, who scripted and directed *Pandora and the Flying Dutchman* for them, starring James Mason and Ava Gardner. Their second deal was with Horizon Pictures—later with a new Spiegel incorporation called Horizon Enterprises—to make *The African Queen*. It was an old C. S. Forester novel that had nearly been filmed twice, once with Elsa Lanchester and Charles Laughton, and once with Bette Davis and David Niven. John Huston was enthusiastic about the story of a hard-bitten riverboat man and an American missionary going downstream to blow up a German warship on Lake Victoria. As Horizon Pictures was heavily in debt over *We Were Strangers*, Spiegel had no money to buy the property from Warner Brothers, but he secured a verbal option on it.

To provide operating capital, Spiegel mortgaged his house on Crescent Drive for $25,000 and gave the man who held the mortgage 5 percent of the new film's possible profits. Then he began to use his talents as a packager. He gave the book to Katharine Hepburn to read and told her that he had Huston to direct and Humphrey Bogart to star in it. He then told Huston to take Bogart out and get him to play the leading role. "The hero is lowlife," Huston said. As Bogart was the biggest lowlife in town, he was the most suitable for the part. After drinking at Romanoff's, they both went to see Hepburn and convince her to act in the film. Then Spiegel went to Sound Services Incorporated, which supplied sound equipment to the studios, and persuaded its directors to lend him the $50,000 he needed to buy the property in return for his undertaking to use their equipment on location and to give them credits along with Bogart, Hepburn and Huston.

It was Spiegel at his best, using one name to attract another and investment. United Artists was being taken over from its film-star owners, Charles Chaplin and Mary Pickford, by Arthur Krim and Robert Benjamin on a loan provided by the brilliant Chicago financier Walter E. Heller. It needed product to distribute. Once Spiegel had secured a deal with the Woolf brothers to shoot *The African Queen* in England, with Romulus Films putting up all the production costs below the line—for technicians and equipment and laboratories—he went to Heller and secured an agreement that Heller would fund all the costs above the line for the writers, the director, the producers and the stars, in return for the American distribution rights to the film. Through Horizon Enterprises, Spiegel himself would provide a bond that would guarantee the completion of the picture. Bogart was only going to receive $35,000 in cash with $125,000 as a deferred payment plus 25 percent of the film's profits. Hepburn was in for $130,000 plus 10 percent of the profits, while Huston was to take $87,000 and half the profits of Horizon Pictures, the parent company of the new Horizon Enterprises. Spiegel's own producer's fee was deferred, but his expenses were not and they would be gargantuan.

Huston had been making *The Red Badge of Courage* with Spiegel's rival, Gottfried Reinhardt, as the producer. The film was harrowing and difficult to make. It would turn out to be as bruising and gallant and destructive as the Civil War. Meeting Spiegel at the time, Reinhardt told him that *The Red Badge* would be a great picture. "*The African Queen* will make a lot of money," Spiegel replied. Yet the problems of the screenplay had not yet been solved. John Huston insisted on engaging the leading film critic James Agee to work with him on the script. He whisked Agee away to an athletic regime at a country club near Santa Barbara, which eventually gave Agee a heart attack after he had completed half his work on the screenplay. Agee was a bottle-a-day drinker and a chain-smoker. "I wouldn't call it self-destructiveness, but carelessness," Huston said of him. "He didn't give his corporeal self any thought." As it was, Agee almost proved Henry Ford's dictum that you did not need exercise if you were well, but if you were ill, it would kill you, although Agee himself survived for a few more years. The conclusion of the draft screenplay was pessimistic, leaving the hero and heroine dead as in most of Huston's pictures. Self-destructive himself, Huston did not believe in happy endings.

Spiegel tried to make Huston alter the final scenes by persuading the new screenwriter, Huston's old collaborator Peter Viertel. "It's downbeat.

It has no lift. It will be just another wonderful financial failure," Spiegel told Viertel, who reported the conversation in his *roman à clef* called *White Hunter, Black Heart*. Huston needed a hit. The banks were beginning to be leery of his artistic failures like *We Were Strangers*. Viertel did not need another flop himself. So he heard the siren songs from Vine Street and Sunset Boulevard about the necessity for an upbeat ending and convinced Huston that one would be artistic as well as essential. He had been spiegelized.

Huston was little help to Spiegel in London with the Woolf brothers. He seemed to enjoy creating problems that imperiled the whole coproduction. Spiegel complained that Huston nearly killed the deal five times, but Spiegel worked like a dog to keep it going. At first, Huston refused to shoot the picture in color, because he had never shot in color before. His British cameraman, Jack Cardiff, was an expert in color photography, the best in the business, and Huston had nothing to fear. Then he insisted on going to Africa to find an ink-black river to prove his preference for black and white. Instead he found the Ruki River, a tributary of the Congo with lush green tropical jungles, which converted him to the idea of color. After months on location trips in Africa, he refused to shoot in Kenya, which was a sterling area that did not break British regulations about exporting currency overseas. He chose remote sites in Uganda and the Belgian Congo, where banking and communications and logistics were difficult to arrange. It was almost as if he were making the film impossible for the producers to finance.

He took pleasure in needling his partner in Horizon Pictures. At the first production dinner for the American and British producers and the chief technicians, he decided that he would embarrass Spiegel, who still might support the British and have the film made mainly in England to comply with the law. The Woolf brothers did not know the story behind shooting *The Invader* with Buster Keaton in 1935, but Huston did. He shouted to Spiegel that they had never operated in London together before. Spiegel uneasily agreed. Huston proposed a toast. "Let's drink to Old Bailey." Everyone drank, laughing, but Spiegel stopped eating. He was still humiliated by his first experience of filming in London, and feared that the Woolf brothers would hear of it. "Hungry," Huston said, watching Spiegel lay down his fork, "but he can't eat."

The British producers were having their own troubles raising their half of the budget of one million pounds. They had been to Alexander Korda with the script and he had advised them that they were making a mistake. "A story of two old people going up and down a river. You will be bankrupt." The National Film Finance Corporation, which was putting up a fifth of the British production costs, was advised by Michael Balcon of Ealing Studios that *The African Queen* did not qualify as a British picture, even though it was to be made with British technicians and in a British studio. It had two American stars and an American director and co-producer. The production deal broke down completely when Spiegel could not produce a completion bond that would cover the risks of filming with Hollywood stars in the depths of Africa. Heller refused to pay for the salaries of Hepburn and Bogart, who was already flying to London with his wife Lauren Bacall.

It was an extraordinary crisis, and Spiegel rose to the occasion. Danger seemed to stimulate him. Risk and the prospect of ruin were his adrenalin. Huston said he liked Spiegel because he was such a desperate man, while Viertel admired him for his sad continental grace and polish, which he maintained despite surviving pogroms in his youth and Nazis in his later days. Spiegel put up Hepburn and Bogart and Bacall in style at Claridge's and began renegotiating their contracts. Bogart was now to get no cash, with all of his $160,000 deferred until the picture began to make money: his share of the profits rose to 30 percent. Even Hepburn said that she would defer half her $130,000. But the catch was that nothing was to be paid at all until Spiegel had settled the financial problems. There was even some doubt that he could pay the hotel bill for the stars. Hepburn would not accept that. She said that she had lived in a lot of worse places than Claridge's and she was too tight to get stuck with the bill. "If you don't have the money, Sam, say so." Spiegel had, however, persuaded the hotel manager to give him credit, and the stars stayed on at Claridge's until they flew off to Africa. "I didn't mind doing the film for nothing," Hepburn said later, "but I didn't intend to pay money for the privilege of doing it."

Both the British and American producers were too committed not to come to a solution. Spiegel had counted on that. If the film were to be called off, both parties would each lose half a million dollars. The British gave way and produced the completion bond, which Spiegel could not find. Walter Heller then honored his obligation and paid the money due for the writers, the stars and Spiegel's expenses. The picture could begin shooting on the locations chosen by Huston: at Butiaba on the shores of Lake Albert in Uganda, at the Murchison Falls, and on the Ruki River in the Belgian Congo, where a whole village compound was built from palm leaves and raffia, surrounded by trenches filled with kerosene in case of attack by soldier ants. Huston believed in actors suffering during location shooting. "Their very hardships give character to the finished film."

Huston now caused fresh problems for the production. He not only seemed to thrive on crisis, but to have Hemingway on the brain. He decided that he was really a big game hunter. He wanted particularly to bag an elephant. He disappeared for weeks at a time with a scarred tracker called Mascota, looking for an old bull to shoot. Finally, he had to admit he never killed an elephant, although he surely tried. "I never got a shot at one whose trophies were worth the crime. No, not crime, sin." Katharine Hepburn, who was persuaded to go shooting with Huston during the filming, gave another reason. "He couldn't hit a tin can with a peashooter, but he liked to give the impression he could kill an elephant."

Huston was off shooting in the bush, when Spiegel and the stars and the film crew flew to Stanleyville in the Belgian Congo. Torrential rain was pouring down. Nothing seemed to be prepared. Everybody was complaining and ready to fly back home. Spiegel was again in his element, showing his usual control and elegance. To Viertel, Spiegel became the one hero, "a perspiring Napoleon planning his hundred days." He held continual meetings with the British technicians, to hear their complaints about impossible working conditions and the failure to get tea, eggs and bacon in the Congo. He organized a dinner of champagne and caviar for the actors to prove that civilization extended to the heart of Africa, while there was still food rationing in England. He was a master at organizing air and train timetables and the departure of trucks and equipment. He even saw that people received their spending allowances in local currency. As a diplomat and an organizer, he was superb. And the skies cleared, as if he had commanded them.

The company reached the compound beside the Ruki River by wood-burning train, jeep and raft. Huston met them, sporting a dinner jacket and an English accent and a monkey on his shoulder, as if he were a hunter on safari. The rains began again, to his delight, and he left Spiegel and the crew to chase after his elephant. Not until the fifth day did the sun shine and shooting begin. Spiegel was in despair and thought that Huston needed a straitjacket for his decision to film in the wettest spot on earth; but Huston had what he wanted, jungle conditions of great discomfort to force the performances he needed from his stars.

Bogart and Hepburn both came from similar backgrounds of social standing. Bogart, in particular, was the opposite of the film roles he played—actually a man of urbanity and sophistication, who loved the city and hated rough life in a palm hut. He and Bacall lived on scotch and even brushed their teeth in it, so avoiding the dysentery that affected everyone else except the hard-drinking Huston. Even the mosquitoes that bit him, Bogart said, rolled over dead or drunk.

Hepburn, however, saw herself as an antelope, "swift, lean, graceful (I hope) and freckled." She took to the primitive life to the manner unborn. She was converted to shooting game for the pot by Huston, who called her "a Diana of the hunt" for her skill with her little Mannlicher rifle and her lack of fear. He also called her "the Jeanne d'Arc of Ruki" for her energy and determination in leading the fight against an attack by soldier ants on the compound. Only once did she jib—at plunging into a river infested with large crocodiles. Huston offered to have a few rounds fired into the water to scare off the beasts. "What about the deaf ones?" Hepburn asked, and then did the shot among the papyrus reeds.

The core of the story of *The African Queen* lay in the comic war between the two misfits, Bogart and Hepburn, with her famous rebuke of his drunkenness, "Nature, Mr. Allnutt, is what we are put into this world to rise above." Bogart was not playing his usual role of a tough detective or criminal, but a wretched, sleazy, absurd, brave little man. He got into the skin of it as Hepburn did into the skin of the lady missionary. On the first day of shooting, John Huston visited Hepburn at breakfast. She told him not to make it a habit, she preferred to eat alone. She also said that she was worried about how she might look on screen with her hollow and serious face, her strong jaw and her mouth that went down. "If I can smile," she said, "I've a lot of nice teeth. I can cheer everything up quite a lot."

So Huston asked her if she had ever seen Eleanor Roosevelt in newsreels while she was visiting the war-wounded in hospitals. Then he drifted off. Hepburn thought it was the most brilliant suggestion. "Because she was ugly she always smiled. So I smiled. Otherwise he said very little to me on the set." Hepburn played the part of the dowdy missionary lady with a nervous smile flashing on and off to hide her shyness and determination. Bogart commented on her character to the press, "Brother, your brow goes up. Is this something from *The Philadelphia Story*?" But he could not undercut the comic edge that whetted their opposed performances, and received an Oscar to prove himself wrong.

Huston showed great ingenuity in filming under the difficult conditions that he had inflicted upon everybody. The *African Queen* was a genuine reconstructed riverboat and towed three rafts behind it. On the first were the cameras and camera crew to shoot the ship's progress; on the second, the rest of the film equipment, the props and the lights; on the third, a generator to power the lights and the camera. A fourth raft, built on oil drums for Hepburn's private dressing room and toilet, proved the last straw that broke the *African Queen's* engine and had to be left beside the bank. The worst crisis was when the riverboat sank at its moorings one night. Huston managed to reach Spiegel in London by radio telephone. "I thought you said the *African Queen* sank," Spiegel said, not believing his ears. When he was told that it had gone down, he only said, "Oy!"

It took the crew and two hundred Congolese workers three days to refloat the riverboat and two more days to start its engine. As the film was now over schedule, Spiegel flew out for a consultation, only to be bitten on the back of the neck by a huge and poisonous spider. Bacall was carrying supplies of the new wonder-drug penicillin with her. Massive doses of antibiotics saved Spiegel. Both Bacall and Hepburn had been looking after the crew for months—"a couple of Florence Nightingales" the second-unit cameraman Ted Scaife called them. Huston did not want Spiegel on location dead or alive. He persuaded the local village chief, called King Paul, to organize a hundred Congolese, beating drums and chanting, "Welcome Sam," whenever Spiegel tried to call a production conference. Spiegel left after helping Huston plan the transfer of the *African Queen*, the equipment, the crew and the actors to Butiaba in Uganda, before completing the location sequences near the Murchison Falls.

Dysentery and malaria and other sicknesses cut short the necessary filming in Africa. Nine members of the crew had to be sent back to England. Huston wanted to shoot on, but was faced with a mass revolt from his actors, technicians and producers. He had to accept a return to Isleworth Studios to complete some of the African sequences on the back lot and at Worton Hall, where the famous shots with Bogart and the leeches were filmed. Huston tormented his star for weeks, saying that Bogart would have to put live leeches on his bare legs, or he wouldn't shudder properly when Katharine Hepburn removed them with boric powder. More than that, Bogart would be in breach of contract if he did not perform with real leeches: Spiegel backed Huston in this assertion. A professional breeder of leeches and mosquitoes was brought in to provide the specimens. But at the last moment, rubber leeches were attached to Bogart's skin, while the breeder himself provided the human flesh for the live leech that was shot in close-up. Only legend made Bogart suffer the real thing.

The film was completed for little more than its budget of a million pounds, or four million dollars. It had been a great gamble and a great adventure. Few films at that high cost had been made in such appalling conditions. John Huston had been proved right: the hardships of Africa did make the actors give the performances of their lives. *The African Queen* turned out a critical and commercial success all over the world. Spiegel kept a large part of that, because his deal had been hard fought and won. Romulus Films were taking three-quarters of the profits from distribution in the eastern hemisphere, including Europe, while Horizon Enterprises received 25 percent. In the western hemisphere, including the United States, the deal was reversed: Horizon Enterprises took 75 percent and Romulus Films one-quarter of the profits. From these receipts, the actors and the director would receive their shares. As the film was distributed by a third Spiegel corporation, Horizon Productions and Sales Supervision, the receipts from the film were filtered on the way to a sharing of the profits.

Unfortunately, Huston fell out with Spiegel and dissolved their partnership. He was counseled by Bogart's business manager, Morgan Maree, who also became Huston's business manager. Maree had insisted on examining the books of Horizon Pictures to see whether Bogart was receiving his due share of the profits. There were discrepancies, and Bogart was ready to sue Horizon. Huston himself had received only $25,000 for making *The African Queen* and $40,000 for his overtime and no share of the profits to date. Spiegel had merely told him that the statements were taking a long time to process. Maree met Huston in Paris and told him of the details of Spiegel's renegotiations with the stars. Spiegel had also written in huge fees for a "producer's representative," probably himself, to verify the takings at the theaters. When Maree had reproached him with this plundering, Spiegel had turned to his adviser and said, "I told you we wouldn't get away with this." He did not. Morgan Maree advised Huston to break off all association with Horizon Pictures and Enterprises because they would be involved in legal proceedings. "It was the best-intentioned, worst advice I ever accepted," Huston wrote later, when he had ended his contract with Spiegel for another small sum of $25,000. "No more partnership. No more share of the possible profits." *The African Queen* turned out to be one of the most successful pictures Huston ever made—and Spiegel got all the money.

The conflict between Huston and Spiegel was not entirely about money. "Both had an inner core of strength about what they believed in," Max Youngstein said. "They avoided that confrontation for longer than I expected." They had not worked well together on *The African Queen*, and Huston decided to cut Spiegel out of another deal with the Woolf brothers. Huston wanted to make *Moulin Rouge*, with José Ferrer in the role of the crippled French painter Toulouse-Lautrec. He and Jimmy Woolf flew to New York, bought the film rights to the book and arranged another distribution deal with United Artists, leaving Spiegel out in the cold.

Spiegel seemed to spend all of his nights in London clubs or playing gin rummy with fellow Central Europeans, usually watched by a stray beautiful girl leafing through the pages of the *Hollywood Reporter*. His apartment in Grosvenor Square, leased from a maharajah, was filled with antique mirrors and large beds. It became a watering hole for all the Hollywood people who were visiting London, because rationing did not seem to affect the food and liquor available—only the heating. Spiegel himself never seemed to rise from his bed until noon and was always late for production meetings. And he wanted to make a film called *Melba* about the opera singer, written by his friend Harry Kurnitz. Neither the Spiegel style nor the movie subject appealed to the Woolfs and they threw in their lot with Huston, preferring his reckless talent to Spiegel's prodigal life-style.

Spiegel did not yet have any of the profits from *The African Queen*. While he could still count on his distribution deal with United Artists, which was prepared to invest in *Melba*, he had lost his British backing. Once again he used his contacts with the British aristocracy (although not the same ones from his debacle over *The Invader*), particularly the Honorable Penelope Dudley Ward. Her mother had been the close friend of the Prince of Wales before Lady Furness and Wallis Simpson, and she was to marry the English director Sir Carol Reed. Through her, Spiegel was introduced to potential backers, in particular Lord Grantley, a film producer who had helped many young men into the business including Ivan Foxwell, later the producer of *The Colditz Story*, whom he plucked from oblivion among the technicians in a transatlantic liner with the remark, "Gentlemen are not camera assistants."

Grantley did not believe in the truism that you could not be in Debrett and in the film industry. Spiegel had to endure a weekend of chill privation in Grantley's stately home during the last weeks of rationing and fuel cuts. He returned, blue with cold and hungry and without a penny of investment, to have dinner with his old friend Lady Cook, soon to marry the English director Terence Young. Asked whether he had enjoyed his weekend with the aristocrats, Spiegel said, "What do you expect from these shabby gentiles?" Then he kissed Lady Cook, who had not forgotten his sale of her first editions of George Bernard Shaw. "Darling," Spiegel said, "It's been more than seven years, and there is the statute of limitations. I don't owe you any money."

These were the last years when the stories of Spiegel's hustling were recorded. *The African Queen* quickly grossed ten times more than its cost and is still bringing in money for Horizon Pictures. That meant an income for Spiegel of half a million dollars a year for several years after 1952, and lesser amounts thereafter. He could now afford his life-style and his generosity. No longer could he be characterized in London as the man who attended an air force reunion dinner with an air marshal at the Savoy Grill, paid for everybody with a check, received half the amount in cash from the air marshal, who then had to pay for the whole bill when Spiegel's check bounced. Nor could the story be told of Spiegel walking down a London street with a beautiful woman on his arm, when somebody kicked him violently from behind. Without turning, Spiegel said, "The check is in the mail." And walked on.

He could also afford to ride out his biggest flop, the film *Melba*. He hired Lewis Milestone to direct, remembering the masterpiece that he had helped to distribute in Germany, *All Quiet on the Western Front*. He worked a great deal on the screenplay with Harry Kurnitz: its final version was characterized by Bosley Crowther as "a mere offense to the taste and credulity of the average numbskull." Unfortunately, Spiegel injected into the story of the Australian diva's career all his favorite pieces of opera and song. Dame Nellie Melba, played by the Metropolitan Opera singer Patrice Munsel, belted out "Comin' Through the Rye" in her opening number in front of Queen Victoria, then followed it with "Ave Maria," "Caro nome" from *Rigoletto*, the mad scene from *Lucia di Lammermoor*, and snatches from *The Daughter of the Regiment*, *The Barber of Seville*, *Tosca*, *La Bohème*, *La Traviata*, *Lohengrin*, *Romeo and Juliet*, and a terminal rendering of "On Wings of Song." It was a quick Cook's Tour through the operatic repertoire, or as Crowther called it, "a massive mélange of mighty music." Even Lewis Milestone said the script was worthless. The film had nothing to do with Dame Nellie. "It should have been called *Melba* like I should have been christened Napoleon."

There was, moreover, a lavishness in the production which only embellished its mediocrity. Milestone refused to shoot in a small studio and used London interiors—five sets were found in an old Rothschild building in Fire Lane across the way from the Dorchester Hotel. There was a scale and a sumptuousness in *Melba* that suggested a later Spiegel style. He had a great deal to do with the look of the film. "When he meddled in the production himself," Gottfried Reinhardt said of Spiegel, "it was always a disaster." He needed strong and brilliant directors like John Huston, Elia Kazan and David Lean. Even his friend Max Youngstein at United Artists blamed Spiegel for the flop. "No other man could have pulled off the stunt of turning out a piece of absolute garbage like *Melba*." Its failure led to a break between Spiegel and the president of United Artists, Arthur Krim, who ended by yelling at Spiegel, "You can jump out of the window and get killed." It seemed the end of Spiegel's winning streak. Then a young film accountant, Douglas Gosling remembers Spiegel interviewing him for a job while his office furniture was being carried into the street by the bailiffs. Reclining on a repossessed *chaise longue* on the sidewalks of Mayfair, Spiegel assured Gosling that he could work for Horizon Pictures on the next film.

CHAPTER SEVEN

The Eagle Folds Its Wings

Professional is one thing, politics is another. Separate them.

SPIEGEL

Spiegel was a man who worked on his luck, good or bad. With his removal to London to make *The African Queen*, his marriage and his finances in California became unstuck. Left on her own, Lynn Baggett took to drink and cruising. "She was in a battling relationship with Sam," Mary Anita Loos said. "She didn't like him, but she couldn't let him go. She was very beautiful, but she did not have class." Spiegel had essentially abandoned her and Hollywood, and he filed for divorce in Santa Monica in October 1952. The suit charged his wife with adultery and cruelty and asked the court to grant Spiegel the divorce and declare that there was no community property. Spiegel asserted that he and Lynn had not lived together for eighteen months, and that she had committed adultery with various persons known to Spiegel, and that she had treated him in an extremely cruel and inhuman manner, causing him bodily pain and mental anguish.

Lynn Baggett countersued on the same grounds of adultery and cruelty. She claimed that she had been abandoned and left destitute. Her husband's worth was between two and three million dollars, one million dollars of which were community assets in his control. She asked for her debts of $15,000 to be paid and maintenance of $3,000 monthly to be granted. In the event, Spiegel's assets were nowhere near as much as his wife contended. His accountant agreed that the amount came to $622,000, but Spiegel owed the federal government $273,000 in back taxes, and the government had a lien of $20,000 against his home on Crescent Drive. As it was, Internal Revenue Service agents soon seized Spiegel's house under a warrant to pay off tax debts owing since 1946, thus ending his residence in Beverly Hills.

Worse was to happen to the unlucky Lynn Baggett. She was awarded alimony of only five hundred dollars a month, and she became involved in a fatal road accident. Driving a yellow Nash Rambler station wagon loaned to her by the actor George Tobias, she crashed into another station wagon on the corner of Orlando and Waring Avenues. In the other car were five children and two adults returning from a beach outing. One little boy was killed and another seriously injured. Lynn Baggett jumped out of her station wagon, looked at the victims lying in the road, jumped back into her car and sped away. The following day, she was arrested and charged on suspicion of a felony. She was acquitted of manslaughter, but was sent to jail for fifty days for hit-and-run driving. Of all the friends who had accepted her and her husband's prodigal hospitality, Radie Harris noted, only one remembered to send her in jail a message of good cheer on New Year's Eve.

Spiegel did nothing to help the wife he was divorcing during her trial and time in prison. He was making his next important film, *On the Waterfront*, in New York. The opportunity had been created by him working on his good luck. As he had lost his house in Crescent Drive, he was staying at the Beverly Hills Hotel. He had left the door of his suite open, either to admit one of his passing women or to overhear a crisis proceeding in the next suite, where Elia Kazan and Budd Schulberg had been turned down by most of the studios with their project *On the Waterfront*. There were many reasons for the diffidence of the Hollywood chiefs. The subject of the screenplay was racketeering and union politics among the longshoremen in New York. Still smarting from the Bioff and Brown blackmail scandal, which had resulted in both labor racketeers and the head of a studio serving jail sentences, Hollywood wanted no picture on that sore subject. It was also afraid of the powerful Teamsters Union, which was closely allied to the longshoremen. Politically, Kazan and Schulberg seemed to have written a personal justification and atonement. Both had named fellow writers and filmmakers as Communists to the House Un-American Activities Committee. To the Hollywood Ten condemned to jail and unemployment, *On the Waterfront* was a film designed to justify stool pigeons and slander trade unionism.

Arthur Miller had originally been working on a film script about politics among the longshoremen, "The Hook," which was killed by Columbia Pictures after he refused the suggestion of Harry Cohn and the Federal Bureau of Investigation that he should substitute Reds for racketeers on the waterfront. The eventual Schulberg version of the script did create a conflict about the ethics of informing. For instance, a dead bird was thrown at the informer Terry Malloy's feet with the bitter remark, "A pigeon for a pigeon." Kazan denied that the film was a defense of his naming names, even though Zero Mostel always called him "Looselips." Certainly Terry Malloy is presented almost as a Christ in the Judas role of the betrayer who becomes a labor hero and martyr. In the film, to testify is like giving witness at a Quaker meeting or being born again. When the film was actually shot in winter on location in Hoboken on the docks, Kazan was surrounded by locals and longshoremen. "It was like a public trial," he said. He never would finally explain his motives in testifying to the House Un-American Activities Committee. He would quote Jean Renoir's favorite remark, "Everyone has his reasons."

Paradoxically, Spiegel had been employing those who had been blacklisted. Now he would employ those who were partially responsible for confirming the names on the blacklist. He walked through the open door of the suite in the Beverly Hills Hotel, where Kazan and Schulberg were discussing their woes. He was wearing an elegant midnight-blue suit and smelling of lilacs. He invited the two men to a party in his suite and asked them if they were in trouble. They began to tell him that they were. Darryl Zanuck had said of the script: "What you have written is exactly what the American people don't want to see." Spiegel cut them off. They could tell him the story tomorrow. As Schulberg was flying off early, Spiegel promised to leave his door unlocked so he would not have to get up to open it.

In his afterword to the published screenplay of *On the Waterfront*, Schulberg left an unforgettable portrait of Spiegel.

> *Spiegel had gone down as often as Primo Carnera. But he had gotten up more often. With his keen mind, courtly manners (to those he courted), and sybaritic tastes, he was a very special kind of Wandering Jew, a throwback to the days when pirates were heroes if they were YOUR pirates. When he was up he was very up and when he was down he knew the Hollywood and Middle-European game of behaving even more successfully.*

The next morning, Schulberg walked into Spiegel's room, where the producer lay inert beneath his sheets. The writer paced around the room telling the story of the film to the comatose Spiegel. He reached the climax and paused. A head appeared. "I'll do it," Spiegel murmured. "We'll make the picture." Or such was Schulberg's version—later denied by Spiegel—of the reading of the screenplay. "I read it that night," Spiegel asserted, "with great difficulty suppressing sleep. It was shockingly bad. . . . I didn't decide to do *Waterfront* on a whim half-asleep in my bed. I wouldn't have touched the original script with a ten-foot pole. I had a difficult time with Budd. He obviously resented that he had to work another year on the rewrite before I would go ahead with the picture.... All of the famous scenes—the one in the taxicab, the one with the pigeons—were new, and the theme itself was entirely different."

Spiegel would not leave the script alone. "He went through any amount of walls," Max Youngstein said, "until he got the script he wanted. There was such a contradiction, the way he spoke and moved his hands all over the place. He could have been a caricature of himself, except that what he did turned out at the end to have a touch of perfection." He even taught Kazan a lesson—never to be satisfied with the script that was there. He was always saying: "Let's open it up again." Schulberg found him a hard taskmaster, a bear for structure, also maddeningly manipulative and naturally conspiratorial. He was jealous that Kazan and Schulberg had worked together for so long so closely. He tried to separate them, to speak to them apart, as he did to the stars and technicians. "Divide and rule," Schulberg wrote of Spiegel. "He had to feel that he was in control." He drove Schulberg crazy by demanding yet more changes in the script. Once Schulberg's wife awoke to find her husband dressing at three in the morning saying, "I'm going to New York to kill Spiegel." But in the end, Schulberg thought his script for *On the Waterfront* a model of its kind, embracing five or six significant sequences, each one rushing the action forward and mounting to a climax. But the screenplay paid a price for its narrative drive. Schulberg said it could not wander "as life wanders, or pause as life always pauses, to contemplate the incidental or the unexpected."

Yet it was the incidental or the unexpected that helped the film to be financed and made. Frank Sinatra was first approached to play the lead role of Terry Malloy. He accepted, but his name was not big enough at the time to secure the budget of nine hundred thousand dollars needed to make the picture. Marlon Brando's name was big enough, and he had worked with Kazan on Tennessee Williams's *A Streetcar Named Desire*, but Kazan's naming of names had caused a breach between them. Spiegel did not know how to get to Brando. Unable to sleep, he was in the famous Seventh Avenue Stage Delicatessen in midtown Manhattan at three o'clock in the morning, when Brando walked in off the streets. Spiegel told him the story of the latest version of *On the Waterfront*, and Brando caught fire, but still refused to work with Kazan. "Professional is one thing," Spiegel said, "politics is another. Separate them."

Spiegel then called Kazan on the telephone in the early hours of the morning and summoned him to the delicatessen to make his peace with Brando. It was a close thing for half an hour, but Kazan did persuade Brando in the end. He was the best young actor in America and guaranteed the budget—the only young actor who had anything on the old stars, as far as Humphrey Bogart was concerned. "He'll be doing Hamlet," Bogart told the *New York Times*, "when the rest of us are peeling potatoes."

Brando accepted the part and was reconciled with Kazan. Although his usual fee was three times as much, he agreed to play for only $125,000 because he liked the script and knew the picture had a smallish budget. "He believed the picture should be made," Spiegel said, "and he wanted to help." Spiegel then took the project to Columbia Pictures in New York, which had already turned it down twice. This time Spiegel convinced the executives and secured a contract of remarkable independence, which allowed the film to be made on real locations in New York and New Jersey. The head of Columbia, Harry Cohn, did not approve of the project, the contract or the film being made outside a studio. But Spiegel had his way, beginning a long and profitable association with Columbia. He secured 50 percent of the profits from the picture and control over the ancillary rights. "He fought like a tiger for every dime due to him," the Columbia executive Leo Jaffé said. "He was an excellent negotiator."

Frank Sinatra was furious when he heard that he had been replaced by Brando. "Hi, Frank," Spiegel said amiably in a restaurant, only for Sinatra to reply, "You say, Hello, Mr. Sinatra. I prefer if you don't say anything at all." Sinatra complained to his agent, Abe Lastfogel, the head of William Morris, who advised him not to sue. "Do you want the world to know that Hollywood doesn't want you?" Once again, Spiegel had got what he wanted and evaded the consequences of his actions. The casting was completed mainly from the Actors Studio: Rod Steiger and Karl Malden, Lee J. Cobb and Eva Marie Saint. Leonard Bernstein was hired to write film music for the first time in his career, and the expert Boris Kaufman was selected as the cinematographer. If packaging could make a good film, Spiegel would tie the knot. Lee J. Cobb, incidentally, had also behaved like Sterling Hayden, so disgusted with being blacklisted and put out of work that he had named names along with Kazan and Schulberg. His role as the corrupt labor boss, Johnny Friendly, was ironical, for Friendly hated a stool pigeon worse than the devil incarnate or a congressional committee.

During the shooting of *On the Waterfront* in freezing conditions in New

Jersey, Kazan was also ready to kill Spiegel. The shooting schedule was only thirty-five days, with a hostile underworld trying to stop the production. Kazan had police protection, but once he was nearly beaten up. There was corruption, paying off people so that the filming could go on. Kazan fell a day behind schedule. He was on set, a frozen and dingy alley, when Spiegel appeared "in his slick limousine with his compulsory accessory, a lovely lady. The scent of Châteaubriand from *21* was still on their breath." Spiegel told Kazan to make up time, to shoot faster. Kazan said he would quit, but Schulberg talked him back on the job. "We were down to our last out," he told Kazan. "Let's face it, Sam Spiegel saved our ass."

It was the same story at four in the morning in Hoboken, during a scene with Marlon Brando, Eva Marie Saint, Lee J. Cobb and Rod Steiger. "We're frozen," Steiger remembered. "They've got two sun lamps on the camera to keep it from freezing. We're miserable. Spiegel enters and says, 'Good Evening' to us all. He goes outdoors with Kazan and we hear him. 'I don't care what you do. Starve, kill, kick the actors, but get the picture made.' He comes back in, looks at us and says, 'Good Evening.' And he left."

Yet, as in *The African Queen*, the hard conditions and the pressure of work forced extraordinary performances from the actors. Kazan thought Brando as close to genius as anyone he had ever met among actors. Brando had terrific feeling and violence, great intelligence and keen intuition, all hibernating beneath the surface. He did not underact *inside*. His inarticulateness, his sensitivity spoke without words, until these burst out of him in his greatest lines of agony and regret. "You don't understand! I could have been a contender. I could've had class and been somebody. Real class. Instead of a bum, let's face it, which is what I am. It was you, Charley."

It was Spiegel who created the conditions and the class of *On the Waterfront*. He was a creative producer, who put his stamp on all aspects of the production. He now had the courage of his own name and could afford to use it. The credits of *On the Waterfront* showed the producer to be Sam Spiegel. It was a Horizon Picture presented by Columbia, and Spiegel was now Horizon Pictures. S. P. Eagle had been consigned to that pushcart of shady deals and huckster's spiels that Spiegel could now tip on the rubbish dump of past history. "Then, with great bravado," Spiegel said, "I decided it was time to start a new career under my own name."

Kazan had previously come to the same decision when he was told that his name would have more class if he changed it to Cézanne. His protest that there was already a famous painter of that name was answered with: "You make just one good picture and nobody will ever remember the other guy."

When *On the Waterfront* was released in the summer of 1954, it broke box-office records, grossing more than ten times its cost within a year. It also won a record number of Oscars, eight in all, including Spiegel's first Oscar as the producer. It was what the American people wanted to see, and Spiegel was the man with the gall to see that it was made well. It even made cinema history by being the first American film to strike a blow for free speech by including the audacious remark, "Go to hell!" The words were essential dramatically—the industry board censor Joseph Breen said—and served a moral purpose.

Spiegel divorced Lynn Baggett in Santa Monica two months after her release from prison, and the day after *On the Waterfront* had won its eight Oscars. He could be as cruel in success as he could be kind in failure. Before their marriage, he had helped Lynn to secure a part in the Abbott and Costello ghost film, *The Time of Their Lives*: one critic praised her for playing her role "with pleasant and appropriate casualness." In 1950, Spiegel had found her two roles in *D.O.A.* (an abbreviation for "Dead On Arrival"), starring Edmund O'Brien as a man who arrives at a police station expiring from "luminous poison"; and in the swashbuckling *The Flame and the Arrow*, with Burt Lancaster playing the hero as a mixture of Douglas Fairbanks, Senior, and Buster Keaton. But after the divorce, Lynn proved too unstable to pursue her career, which foundered slowly. She became addicted to barbiturates and was trapped for two days in a bed that folded into the wall. She committed suicide in 1960 from an overdose of sleeping pills, a minor Marilyn Monroe.

When S. P. Eagle died, the *New York Times* ran a mock obituary:

This is to mark the passing of S. P. Eagle, who was "born" a full-grown movie producer on a gale of laughter in the steam room of the Fox studio late one afternoon in 1941 and who "died" with a smile of satisfaction and relief two weeks ago in the music dubbing room at Columbia Pictures. The demise of S. P. Eagle was verified after the sneak preview of "On the Waterfront," when it was noted that the film's credits listed the producer as Sam Spiegel. Spiegel and Eagle are, or were, one and the same man. At

*least there is a reasonable certainty shared by Mr. Spiegel, that such was
the case.*

Variety ran a headline on the same subject:THE EAGLE FOLDS ITS
WINGS.

CHAPTER EIGHT

The Bridge on the River Kwai

Never stay in Hollywood more than five days.

SPIEGEL

Just as the coming of sound had given Spiegel the opportunity to enter the movie industry, so the breakdown of the American studio system gave him the chance to become an independent producer based in Europe. In the 1930s the eight major studios—Metro-Goldwyn-Mayer, Universal, Paramount, Warner Brothers, Columbia, Twentieth Century–Fox, RKO and United Artists—had produced almost five hundred films a year, one a week at each of the major studios. But the federal court cases against five of the major studios in the 1950s for conspiring to restrain trade by monopolizing the production, distribution and exhibition of films gave independent producers their chance. The studios had to divorce the production of films from the exhibition of films, while the coming of television made expensive studio productions unprofitable compared with cheaper independent productions. When Humphrey Bogart was asked whether the success of *The African Queen* would stimulate more independent productions in faraway places, he predicted that "not too many years from now the major studios will disappear completely, just serving as outlets for independent productions. That way they'll function nominally, renting out space and players to these new outfits."

It was a trend confirmed by the success of *On the Waterfront*. With his strong new attachment to Columbia Pictures, which was more and more developing independent productions overseas through its London offices headed by Mike Frankovich, Spiegel could afford to develop and finance his future projects from the British capital city. He based himself in his apartment in Grosvenor Square and set up Horizon Pictures in the United Kingdom with offices in Mayfair. He only returned to America for short periods to arrange the financing and distribution of the new pictures that he was making elsewhere. He had no American roots, he told the agent Dennis van Thal, "only permanent refugee status." Meeting the English producer Ivan Foxwell in the Polo Lounge of the Beverly Hills Hotel, Spiegel took care to advise him, "Never stay in Hollywood more than five days." Foxwell had been there for four months, but was flying out to stay at the Plaza in New York the following week. Arriving dog-tired in his hotel room, he soon heard a knock on the door. A pretty girl stood there. "I am Suzy," she said. "I have been sent to you courtesy of Horizon Pictures." To her dismay Foxwell sent her away. Although Horizon Pictures was merely providing the same services that Twentieth Century–Fox had provided for Spiegel on his arrival in New York, Foxwell did not need the gratification.

Spiegel lived his life in compartments. Secretive to a fault, he never allowed the people in one part of his life to meet those in the other parts. His brother was the only exception to the rule. Spiegel proudly introduced Professor Shalom Spiegel to most of his film acquaintances and celebrity friends. Nobody in Hollywood, however, knew that he even had a daughter, Alisa, until she first visited him in Hollywood at the age of seventeen. "He showed you what he wanted," Talli Wyler said. He was the mastermind behind a style of living that was organized as carefully as a resistance movement to the Nazis, with twenty different cells or groups not knowing of one another and only reporting to Spiegel at the top.

His new affluence from the profits of *The African Queen* and *On the Waterfront* encouraged his extravagance and his generosity without curing his old failings. "Once you get into the habit of robbing Peter," Evelyn Keyes said, "I don't think you stop, do you? It's a way of life." Even when Spiegel hired a whole floor of the Connaught Hotel during 1955 and 1956, he would not pay his haberdashers or his tradesmen. Leaving the hotel, Ivan Foxwell went into his shirt maker's nearby. Knowing that he was in the film business, the chief assistant took him to an alcove where twelve tailored suits were hanging on a rack. "Mr. Spiegel," the assistant said, "can have them when he pays for them."

Spiegel also reckoned to pay as few taxes as possible. He set up Horizon Pictures in England as well as in the United States, also in Switzerland and other other tax havens such as the Bahamas and the Cayman Islands. "There were six or seven countries," the Columbia executive Mike Frankovich said, "that he had money in." This series of overlapping companies in various countries enabled the profits from the films to be paid into different accounts in different places, which baffled most of the investigations of the Internal Revenue Service and the Inland Revenue. Spiegel also elected to make his main residence a yacht in the Mediterranean. Ships pay no taxes, only harbor dues. By 1954, Spiegel was already cruising off Capri with Gracie Fields and Noël Coward as his guests. But he had not yet been accepted by the European society he had always wanted to enter.

The following year, the young Czech aristocrat Diana Sternberg (later Phipps) was looking through the telescope mounted on the terrace of the Capri villa of her mother's cousin, Count Bismarck. She saw a large yacht approaching the harbor. She asked the count whose it was. He put the telescope to his eye, then turned to her. "You are not to speak to him," he said. Later, Diana Sternberg saw Spiegel enter the town of Capri wearing a large straw hat with gold chains dangling over his chest and vast stomach. Henchmen ran ahead asking any stray girls in sight to join the film producer aboard his yacht. At Spiegel's approach the streets of Capri emptied of well-brought up young women. Despite his celebrity, they did not wish to meet him.

That was all to change by the late 1950s. The instruments of change were the Kennedys. The father of that remarkable American political clan had himself been a film producer in the days of his notorious affair with Gloria Swanson. He had taught his children the value in politics of show-business connections. Not only was power an aphrodisiac that could attract actresses like Swanson or Marilyn Monroe, but the company of film stars gave an aura of success and glamor to politicians that no amount of campaigning could achieve. The Kennedys, above all, knew how the Hollywood world of celebrities could be mixed with the Washington world of office to dazzle the voters. As Norman Mailer wrote, predicting Camelot before Jack Kennedy was elected to the White House in 1960, "America's politics would now be also America's favorite movie."

Before making the world's favorite movie of 1957, *The Bridge on the River Kwai*, the film that would attract the Kennedys aboard his yacht, Spiegel produced another inconsiderable film for Columbia Pictures, *The Strange One*, with a screenplay by Calder Willingham based on his novel and play *End As a Man*. The point of the book was that the code of honor of a Southern military school fostered the corruption and brutalization of the young cadets, although intended to protect them. As Spiegel himself said, he made the picture as a reaction to most films about juvenile deliquency. "The youngsters were not concerned with knives and guns, but with something far more important and dangerous—insidious ideas." The film, however, became a mere horror story about the evil tricks of Ben

Gazzara, wreaking havoc on the school and his classmates. Although most of the young cast came from the Actors Studio, there was no Brando among them, and their lack of film experience showed. The director, Jack Garfein, performed competently in showing the malevolence and mystery of barracks life, but he underlined the fact that Spiegel's films were good only when the director was very good. Disappointed by the failure of the film, Spiegel removed it from public memory by never referring to it. It had been the same with *Melba*. When making a triumphant speech at the Cannes Film Festival in 1954, Spiegel had claimed a run of two successes. According to him, *On the Waterfront* had followed *The African Queen*. He was interrupted by the witty Hollywood agent, Kurt Frings, shouting to a waiter, "Bring me some burnt toast! Melba!" It was as Budd Schulberg had noticed of Spiegel, when they had first met at the Beverly Hills Hotel. Spiegel had been up with *The African Queen* and was down with *Melba*. "But the way Sam was living it up you would have thought he was celebrating an Oscar winner. . . . If ever anyone knew how to ride out a loser, it was S. P. Eagle."

Two other projects were developed by Spiegel and never made. One was Lion Feuchtwanger's novel about Goya, *This Is the Hour*, to be shot in Spain; the other was Charles Morgan's novel, *The River Line*. But the Pierre Boulle novel about British prisoners of war building for the Japanese *The Bridge on the River Kwai* took precedence over other projects. "It is like holding two tigers by the tail," Spiegel said. "Whichever pulls more strongly will win." He prepared the picture for two years with his usual attention to the script. When asked when he would make the film, he replied with his usual timeless dictum, "When the script is ready." Pierre Boulle was later given sole credit for the screenplay, although he was responsible for little of it. He was covering for two writers on the Hollywood blacklist. One of them, the writer and producer Carl Foreman, had bought an option on the book for only three hundred pounds. Alexander Korda turned down the film, saying that the British colonel in the book who built the bridge for the Japanese "death railway" was either insane or a traitor. Spiegel bought the property from Carl Foreman and hired him to write the first draft screenplay without informing Columbia Pictures, because Harry Cohn would never have accepted a screenwriter who was on the blacklist: Cohn did not consider Spiegel even to be a good producer. On Spiegel's advice, Foreman wrote in a part for an American commando, ordered to blow up the bridge. Spiegel wanted Humphrey Bogart to play the role, but Bogart was already committed to another production for Columbia, and Cohn would not release him. The situation was made worse by Spiegel hiring a second writer on the blacklist to do another draft, Michael Wilson, because Foreman returned to the United States to clear himself with the House Un-American Activities Committee. Both Foreman and Wilson later complained that they had been cheated of an Oscar and a credit for the screenplay, but neither was in any position to demand his name on the credits. Spiegel was good to risk losing his studio financing by hiring their talents—and Foreman was given a posthumous Oscar for his work.

In fact, by using writers suspected of Communist sympathies, Spiegel himself earned a dossier in the Federal Bureau of Investigation. The numerous entries in it have all been deleted for security reasons except for one sentence in a memorandum sent by J. Edgar Hoover, the Director of the Bureau, to the American Embassy in Paris, dated December 14, 1954. "Spiegel has in the past (*deleted*) although it was never definitely determined that he was acting as an espionage agent for the Russians." Such an allegation only demonstrated official suspicion of Spiegel's background and contacts, not of his loyalty to his adopted country.

Disillusioned by using an unknown director for *The Strange One*, Spiegel sought the best for his new project. He considered Howard Hawks and John Ford, but he settled on the English director David Lean, whose wartime films such as *In Which We Serve* showed his admirable grasp of the British military mind, at least as represented by Noël Coward playing a surrogate Lord Mountbatten. As usual with those whom Spiegel hired cheaply, Lean was down on his luck. He had even sold his gold cigarette case and rang Spiegel in desperation to ask for a job. "Spiegel was very good at helping talented people at their lowest moment," Ivan Foxwell commented. "It established a debt of gratitude." Lean remembered differently, having arrived broke in New York, being given the Boulle book to read by an agent and accepting to direct the film as long as the screenplay was rewritten. "The whole film started in an American submarine," he said. "The thing was being depth-charged. It really was not very good." He himself rewrote it with Michael Wilson, after a disastrous intervention by Spiegel's previous screenwriter, Calder Willingham, who was sent out to Ceylon to work on a new draft with Lean. Columbia's head of overseas production, Bill Graf, read Willingham's work and had him airborne back to London before Spiegel was even notified. "We finally did it," Lean said of the script, not admitting to Spiegel's preliminary contributions. Nor did Michael Wilson, who disliked the process of hiring four or five screenwriters so that the producer or director could put his personal stamp on the picture. To him, it displayed insecurity and confusion, not authority and dominance. He knew his wish for a cinema of writers was heresy in film circles, but he could not wait to see the day when the relationship between a screenwriter and a director came close to that between a playwright and a director in the theater. That would not be allowed by Spiegel and Lean until they made their next film together.

There were many changes in the casting of *The Bridge on the River Kwai*. After losing Humphrey Bogart, Spiegel tried for Cary Grant and settled for William Holden. Holden secured an admirable contract, a fee of $300,000 from a total budget of $3,200,000, and also 10 percent of the gross receipts, payable at a maximum of $50,000 a year for tax reasons. Sir Laurence Olivier turned down the part of the correct but maniacal British colonel. He was already committing himself to direct and play in *The Prince and the Showgirl* with an old young friend of Spiegel's. "Why should I go to Ceylon," Olivier asked, "to play a martinet when I can stay at home and act with Marilyn Monroe?" He also did not think that the people of the world wanted to watch a stiff-upper-lipped Englishman spouting out words. David Lean thought of Charles Laughton for the role, but Laughton was too unfit to secure insurance. After that, Lean chose Noël Coward, an idea that was not too absurd after Coward's performance in *In Which We Serve*. Finally, Spiegel settled on Alec Guinness, then known as a comedy actor in Ealing Studio pictures. He had played a leading role with Grace Kelly in the film of *The Swan*, but the picture had not been a success.

Guinness refused the part three times, seeing little interest in the role of the fanatic bridge-builder. He found the original script "rubbish—filled with elephant charges and that sort of thing." Even when the script was revised, he found Colonel Nicholson too blinkered for audiences to take him seriously. Finally, Spiegel invited him out to a restaurant one evening. "I went into that dinner telling Spiegel, 'You're wasting your time,'" Guinness said. "At the end of it, I was asking him, 'What kind of wig will I be wearing?'" Spiegel had persuaded him that the character of the colonel and the script played unconsciously with its own humor. "This," Spiegel said, "was the thing Guinness did not expect."

Sessue Hayakawa, the veteran Japanese actor, also refused to play the camp commandant, but changed his mind in order to work with David

Lean, whom he found solitary and penetrating and solicitous of his actors. Only with Guinness did Lean have trouble, because Guinness knew that Lean would have preferred Charles Laughton in the role. For the first week of shooting, according to Hayakawa, the coolness between Lean and Guinness was "almost solid enough to be seen." But later Guinness came to admire Lean and worked with him many times again. "I suppose we are both strong-willed," Guinness admitted. "And his will is the stronger." But Guinness came to recognize that he owed much of his film career to Lean and only fought with him on three of the six films they made together. His final words on Lean could have been said about Spiegel, "a man of genius cocooned with outrageous charm."

Choosing the location for the film was arduous. Spiegel, Lean and the cameraman Jack Hildyard traveled to the Golden Triangle on the borders of Siam and Burma, but there was no way to carry in film equipment and the real River Kwai turned out to be a trickle. A fine river was found in Malaya, but a guerrilla war was in progress on both banks of it. There was shooting and shooting, after all. In the end, the choice fell on Ceylon, now Sri Lanka, where Bill Graf and Lean found the site for the actual bridge. Spiegel defended the choice of locale. Ceylon, he said, had ideal tropical scenery and the best climate, working and health conditions. "In fact, the countryside was more Siamese in character than the original." As for the unusual subject of the film, Spiegel said that only the unusual interested him. He liked the ambiguity of the subject, British prisoners of war wanting to construct a railway bridge that would benefit the Japanese war effort. "Man came into this world to build," Spiegel said, "and not to destroy. Yet he's thrown into the necessity of destroying, and his everlasting instinct is to try to save himself from having to destroy." There might appear to be no love story in the film, but it was really the greatest love story of all time, "That of men for men in terms of loyalty arrived at through mutual suffering." Anyway, he had a higher opinion of the average audience than most other film producers, who filmed conventional subjects rather than unique ones. One of the greatest faults in the motion picture industry was looking down on the audience. "Never underestimate the taste and intelligence of your audience. They are just as quick to grasp an idea as you are to present it. You set your level; they will meet you there."

So Spiegel justified his expensive production in Ceylon. It took eight months and a quarter of a million dollars to prepare and build the bridge itself. Forty-five elephants dragged fifteen hundred large tree trunks to the site on the river to create a structure 425 feet long and 90 feet high, larger than anything inside Ceylon except the giant tanks at Anuradhpura. Shooting began in October 1956 and continued for eight months until May 1957. During the shooting, the Suez crisis erupted, with the ignominious British invasion of and retreat from the canal zone. The special generator to power the film's lights was on the last ship to slip through the canal before it was blocked. The war crisis seemed a running commentary on the film itself, a dedicated examination of the inflexible military mind, which believed in the superiority of Western methods even if put to the wrong use. Under pressure from the Americans and the Russians, the British retreated from the Suez Canal, but seemed to feel that they were still correct in their actions. Again their attitude was echoed in the film when the Japanese camp commander raged at the British colonel, who was still insisting on his rights. "You are defeated but you have no shame. I hate the English."

David Lean was slow and meticulous in his shooting. He ran over schedule and budget, but he would not accelerate. Spiegel stayed in London or New York, making occasional forays into the field to hurry Lean along. There was a love-hatred between the two men, both dominant, both necessary to each other. "Lean and Spiegel," Jack Hildyard said, "treated each other with respect and animosity." William Holden was another who loved and hated Spiegel. At a party at the Japanese embassy, Holden wrapped a performing king cobra around his neck. It could have bitten him to death. Spiegel shouted at him never to do something so risky while he was filming. He did not give a goddamn what Holden did when the picture was finished. Holden tried to buy the cobra to put in Spiegel's bed. Spiegel would die of a heart attack even if the snake did not bite him. Bill Graf did not agree and said, "I don't think it would even penetrate Spiegel's skin."

Spiegel left most of the production work in Ceylon to the Columbia Pictures production executive Bill Graf, who had the experience, diplomatic skills and toughness to ride out the storms. Graf did not blame Spiegel for staying away to view the rushes in London. "Sam was one of the finest producers the motion picture industry ever had," Graf said. "He was two hundred percent involved in the final product, but he wouldn't sit through a production when it was shooting. It was just too much, too boring. Unless there's a decision to be made, there's nothing for you to do." Graf arranged for superb catering on set, with menus in three national cuisines and food taken up from the cold stores in Colombo every day, only to receive

Spiegel's comment, "I think you're overfeeding the people." But Graf's chief problem was to arrange air transportation in and out of Ceylon. Finally, Spiegel himself intervened, chartering two freight planes from the old military airline Flying Tigers to take the crew and the equipment back at the end of shooting. The problem was that the Flying Tiger Dakotas were often used to transport monkeys to laboratories and stank to high heaven. Spiegel announced the details of the flight home to the crew near Kandy as they were preparing for the climax of the film. He provoked a mass revolt and a joke from David Lean, "I never knew a tiger could fly." Spiegel lost his temper and yelled, "Goddammit, you can find your own way home." In fact, Graf did, canceling one of the Tiger aircraft and stuffing the other with all the equipment, which arrived back aromatic with apes.

The grand finale of the film was the blowing of the bridge with an ancient train and six coaches trundling across it. Five CinemaScope cameras were set up to photograph the explosion, all operated by remote control with the cameramen entrenched in dugouts against the blast. Explosives experts from Imperial Chemical Industries waited by their detonators. A system of control lights had been rigged to warn Lean and Hildyard in their dugout with the master camera that the train and the other four cameras were rolling. After two days of rehearsals, everybody was ready for a take. And Lean and the crew waited for Spiegel to arrive. And waited and waited in the terrible heat. Eventually an air-conditioned limousine drove up. The windows did not come down to let in the force of the hot air. Lean would not go to the limousine and Spiegel would not leave it. Eventually, Spiegel's hand was seen to be raised. Lean ordered the train to start and watched the lights, which would tell him the other four cameras were rolling. One light did not illuminate. Lean stopped the take and the explosion, for there could only be one take and one destruction of the bridge. The train itself jumped the tracks at the far end of the line: it took all night to jack it back onto the track for another attempt next morning.

Spiegel demanded an inquiry into why the take was aborted. It could have cost him the climax of his film. One of the second-unit cameramen had failed to climb from his dugout to switch on the warning light signal and run back to cover. The whole shot had to be restaged, but the second time around, the bridge on the River Kwai blew up in a glorious explosion. When Spiegel was later reproached for his extravagance in building a real railway bridge for a quarter of a million dollars, only to destroy it in half a minute, he said that everything had to be in proportion. There was no story in *Kwai* without a bridge. "And the bridge acquires meaning only when it is destroyed. So you build the bridge to illustrate your point. The question of a quarter of a million dollars is only a number on your cost sheet."

Graf had the footage of the blowing of the bridge guarded by armed men and stored in the safe of the American embassy in Ceylon, for fear that it might be stolen or later opened at customs to check whether the film cans were being used for illicit gem smuggling. They were sent back to the laboratories in London in three separate batches by three different carriers, stored in the pilot's cabin to prevent deterioration of the film stock. Unfortunately, one of the batches did not appear in England, where Spiegel had returned. One week passed; two weeks. Spiegel sent desperate cables, but nobody dared tell him that some of the footage had vanished. Eventually, it was discovered in its cans beside the runway of Cairo airport, perhaps an Egyptian joke to pay back the British for Suez. By a miracle, the unprocessed film was unharmed and all the footage of the explosion was preserved.

The film was completed at Elstree Studios. Malcolm Arnold composed the music, which was played by the Royal Philharmonic Orchestra. Spiegel began fighting with Harry Cohn of Columbia Pictures over the extreme length of the picture. Cohn had never wanted the picture to be made or shot in Ceylon or run that long. He had even tried to cancel the production when Mike Frankovich in the London office had invested $600,000 in preproduction money. The fact that Spiegel had made the film his own way was proof of the growing power of independent producers and the diminishing control exercised by the heads of the Hollywood studios. Spiegel fought for every inch of film to be kept in the final cut of two hours and forty-one minutes that he had approved. In the confrontations that he enjoyed with the executives of Columbia Pictures, he never agreed he was wrong, he never said he would change anything. "His authority came from knowledge and a strong will," the Columbia executive Leo Jaffe said of him. "When he thought he was right, nothing could shake him. He had a one-track mind and artistic control of the picture by contract." In point of fact, Jaffe noticed that suggestions of quality were accepted by Spiegel, but he had to oppose them publicly, then do them later, saying that they were his idea. He could never say that another's suggestion was good and would be used. He had to fight tooth and nail in production meetings, then change his mind privately afterward on his own recommendation to himself.

He had signed a very good contract for *The Bridge on the River Kwai*. Horizon Pictures in its many guises and countries was to split all distribution profits equally with Columbia Pictures, after William Holden had received his 10 percent of the gross receipts. Holden's deferred earnings returned by Columbia totaled more than three million dollars by 1979, which meant that Horizon Pictures would have grossed at least twelve million dollars in the same period of time. From these receipts, Spiegel was to buy himself a penthouse on Park Avenue to make space for his growing collection of French Impressionist paintings. He also wanted to purchase a yacht of his own to act as a permanent base for himself and his offshore operations. In July 1957, Spiegel bought eight paintings for $54,000 from the art collection of a New York banker. Four of them were painted by Van Gogh.

Before the charity premiere of *The Bridge on the River Kwai* in New York in December, Spiegel decided to marry in secret for the third time. He had been seeing a great deal of a leading model, Betty Benson, who was extraordinarily attractive, intelligent and lively, with a taste for wearing men's suits and fedora hats in the Garbo and Dietrich style of the late thirties. She was not particularly domestic, yet nothing could have been farther from domesticity than Spiegel's perambulatory style of life, his nocturnal gambling and his floating homes. He did not tell anyone of his third marriage. When he did confess to it, three weeks after the nuptials, he said to Louella Parsons, "Ah well, marriage like murder will out." He even asked Lady Keith to act as the hostess at a party at the St. Regis after the premiere. Riding up in the elevator to the roof of the hotel, Lady Keith and her friends were joined by the young woman still known as Betty Benson. Lady Keith introduced her as such, only to be told that she was Mrs. Sam Spiegel. Lady Keith had to stand in the receiving line beside Spiegel, who ignored his new wife. He thought Lady Keith knew more important people and would act as a better hostess for the occasion, which proved to be the beginning of the end of Harry Cohn. He suffered a heart attack on his flight home to Los Angeles; the success of *The Bridge on the River Kwai* was to be his only consolation. It won eight Oscars, as had *On the Waterfront*, and added to Columbia Pictures' profits and glory. Spiegel won his second Oscar as the producer of the year's best film. Brilliant was the word Bosley Crowther used to describe the quality of the skills that had gone into making the film, and brilliant was its performance at the box office.

Interviewed in his office after the success of *Kwai*, Spiegel seemed like a cross between a canny producer and a connoisseur. He said the film had only worked because of the long process of preparation. His pictures were usually a literal translation of the script onto the screen. "All the trials and errors of a picture are fought out on paper, and the writing period is for the elimination of doubts. Once confronted by cameras and thousands of people who cost a fortune, you can't have doubts." Preparation was the secret of the success of his major films, and letting people use their imaginations. To reduce a film to the level where everything was clearly stated was offensive to audiences. "The general level of moviegoers has risen much higher than the general level of movie makers." But not in his case, evidently.

CHAPTER NINE

Suddenly Last Spiegel

*Hollywood without Spiegel is like Tahiti
without Gauguin.*

BILLY WILDER

With three major films to his credit, Spiegel found himself an ambassador
of the American cinema. He even returned to Europe and Russia to show
his award-winning films. Other than Mike Todd, the film producer and
the husband of Elizabeth Taylor at that time, Spiegel was the only American
producer to visit Moscow after the signing of the Russo-American cultural
exchange pact in January 1958. "There is tremendous curiosity about our
movies and our way of life among the Russians," Spiegel said, "and there
is obvious suspicion because the people can read only what the Government
wants them to know about us." The right kind of American films shown
in Russia would have more effect on public opinion there than any summit
conference, but they should be films that showed America's pride in its
achievements, not mediocre films that displayed a mediocre culture and
confirmed prejudices that Americans were "warmongers, barbarians or
sexmongers." *On the Waterfront* hardly gave the Russians the impression
of an ethical and uncorrupt United States, although they praised Brando's
performance. *The African Queen* was acclaimed, but *The Bridge on the
River Kwai* surprised them ideologically because they thought that the
colonel played by Alec Guinness should be regarded in England as a traitor.

Traitor was the word used by Spiegel to describe an old friend, who
took his next project from him. After the success of *The Bridge on the River
Kwai*, Otto Preminger was interested in the next novel written by Pierre
Boulle, *The Other Side of the Coin*. When Spiegel jibbed at paying ten
times as much as the pittance he had paid for the rights to *Kwai*, Otto
Preminger intervened with an immediate check for $125,000. As both
producers were working with Columbia Pictures, the money came from
the same source. The incident caused a final breach between Preminger
and Spiegel, who never spoke to each other again. But Spiegel had the last
word, telling Boulle's agent, "I will make sure that this picture is never

made by Columbia." He was as good as his last word.

His alternative choice of a subject was curious. Tennessee Williams had written a shocking short drama called *Suddenly Last Summer*, a fantasy about a homosexual poet torn to pieces and eaten alive by the Spanish street boys he had been approaching. The other elements of the play included maternal incestuous love, insanity and lobotomy. Six months after seeing a performance in New York, Spiegel found himself sleepless on a night flight back to Europe. He read that Patricia Neal was going to play the piece in London. He wondered what the hell would make her do that and became excited and called Tennessee Williams. When Spiegel asked him what he wanted for the movie rights, Williams replied, "How about fifty thousand dollars plus twenty percent of the profits?" For once Spiegel did not bargain after the fiasco on the second Boulle novel. "It's a deal," he said.

Spiegel tried to make the subject sound rather like *The Pilgrim's Progress*. As he told the press, what interested him in the play "was delving and prying into the essence of corruption and depravity and bringing out the moral theme that one cannot abuse other human beings without paying for it either with one's life or sanity." At no point in the film could there be a hint or suggestion that corruption could be pleasurable or that cruelty or immorality might be rewarded. It would be a highly moral motion picture. "The enemies of life are destroyed, the good survive." He also praised the vocabulary of the picture. Audiences would like it. They would hear a kind of language they were not used to hearing on the screen. "Williams is definitely the easiest man on the American ear."

Neither Tennessee Williams nor his fellow screenwriter Gore Vidal saw the filmed play quite as Spiegel did. Both had been told about the dangers of homosexuals preying on Mediterranean boys and being preyed upon by them. Although some of the outspoken homosexuality and cannibalism of the theatrical version was muted because of possible screen censorship, the victim's cousin threatened with frontal lobotomy was made to scream before collapsing, "They ate him!" It was probably the funniest unintentional climax of a film since the famous remark in a Biblical epic, "Beware, the Sodomites are behind you."

Elizabeth Taylor was offered the leading role of the disturbed cousin. Her agent Kurt Frings came from Central Europe and knew how to bargain with Spiegel. He negotiated the highest fee yet paid to a screen actress, half a million dollars, a sum that Elizabeth Taylor was to double for playing Cleopatra. Frings was accused of killing Hollywood by demanding exorbitant prices for his stable of stars. "How can they say that?" he asked. "Hollywood is still here." Taylor had two conditions for playing the difficult role: that the director should be one of her favorite four directors, and that her friend Montgomery Clift should be cast as the strange Doctor Cukrowicz, her doctor in the film. She had twice before worked with Clift and preferred to ignore the fact that he could hardly now perform with his scarred face, alcoholism, drug-taking and depressions. With Joseph Mankiewicz chosen as the director because of his success with *All About Eve*, Elizabeth Taylor had the people she wanted to make the film.

The outsiders were Spiegel and his second choice of the second lead actress, Katharine Hepburn. Spiegel had first wanted Vivien Leigh, but her personal problems were too great to allow the casting. Katharine Hepburn had her own troubles. Spencer Tracy was ill and she did not want to leave him in America to film in Shepperton Studios, where Spiegel claimed that Oliver Messel could construct a mansion from the Deep South; and she had been deceived by Spiegel into thinking George Cukor would direct, not Mankiewicz, who had caricatured her shamelessly in *All About Eve*. She also had strong ideas on how to play her lurid material, which Mankiewicz would not accept. She wanted to act in different styles, low and medium and high key, then have the best take chosen when the rushes were shown. Mankiewicz insisted that she play the scenes his way, with an elegant hauteur. She did not always heed him. Once he told her that he would close down the production until the Directors Guild card, which he had ordered for her, arrived from Hollywood. She stormed off the set, but was professional enough to resume shooting the next day.

One of the other leading actresses in the production, Mercedes McCambridge, said that everyone connected with the film was unhappy. "The ambience and the vibrations were terribly upsetting." Mankiewicz became so nervous that he developed a skin rash and had to wear white gloves during shooting. He combined with Elizabeth Taylor in defending Montgomery Clift, who could hardly deliver his lines and was giving one of the worst performances of his life. When Spiegel saw the rushes, he told Taylor that he would have to fire Clift. "Over my dead body," Taylor said. Spiegel now found himself banned from the set by Taylor and Mankiewicz, conspiring to protect Clift from his wrath. A replacement was sought in secret, but the screen test of the little-known actor Peter O'Toole ended in disaster. Asked to pretend to be a doctor performing an operation,

O'Toole turned to face the camera and Spiegel, before ad libbing, "It's all right, Mrs. Spiegel, your son will never play the violin again." Spiegel's rage was incandescent. He swore that O'Toole would never, but never, work for him. He was a bad prophet, but Montgomery Clift kept his role in *Suddenly Last Summer*.

Spiegel hired a white 120-foot pleasure cruiser, which he moored at Palamós near the locations for the film. He always cared about places, which gave a picture "a certain added halo—it's like what Renoir did to his peaches." These particular locations had been recommended by Evelyn Keyes, who had married the clarinet player Artie Shaw and lived above Bagur on the Spanish coast. Before her new marriage, she had had a long affair with the producer Mike Todd, who had then married Elizabeth Taylor, now married to Eddie Fisher, in the usual merry-go-round of love that seemed to pass for lifelong romance in Hollywood. Spiegel himself never visited the Shaws' house, greeting Evelyn Keyes on his yacht, dressed in white shorts and a captain's cap, his full belly jutting forward. "He had his usual gorgeous redhead, blonde and brunette with him." Artie Shaw himself was immune to Spiegel's famous charm. "There is nobody in the whole world who wins everybody," Keyes said. "You have to be amused at what the Sam Spiegels of the world do before you like it. If not, you could hate it." Spiegel rarely left the yacht, surveyed the shooting from afar, saw the rushes nightly and brooded on his revenge.

Katharine Hepburn also plotted her revenge. When Mankiewicz finally wrapped up the shooting in England, Hepburn asked him if he was sure that he did not need her services anymore, "Yes," he said, "I'm sure." She put her face close to his and spat in his eye. Then she strode into Spiegel's office in Shepperton Studios and asked him the same question. She received the same answer and spat in Spiegel's eye. "It's rather a rude gesture," she admitted later, "but at least it's clear what you mean." It was not clear to Spiegel. It had often happened to him before. Kay Harrison, the vice-president of Technicolor, thought him the most amazing man she had ever seen. People came up and literally spat in his face. "He took out a sixteen-inch monogrammed handkerchief, wiped the spit off, smiled and went on trucking. That's the way he was."

Spiegel never worked again with his three stars, Hepburn and Taylor and Clift, nor with his director. Mankiewicz had the right to the first cut of the film by contract, but when Spiegel saw the "director's cut," he had Mankiewicz banned from Shepperton Studios and completed the film himself. He also had Mankiewicz's name struck off all the film's publicity material unless Mankiewicz had a contractual right to be mentioned. It was unwise to try to exclude Spiegel from a Spiegel film.

In spite of the taboo subject and the fact that *Suddenly Last Summer* was one of the unhappier pictures ever made, its notoriety created a success at the box office, where it took more than $13,000,000, and was a partial success with the critics. *Time* magazine might call the film a homosexual fantasy of guilty pleasure and pleasurable punishment with the dead hero "no more than a sort of perverted Peter Pan, and the cannibalism itself nothing more than an aggravated case of nail-biting." But there was considerable respect for Elizabeth Taylor's intense emotional performance, particularly when a gigantic close-up of her flawless face was superimposed over the final shots of the bestial death of her cousin.

At the end of the shooting, Spiegel gave one of his rare interviews to the sympathetic writer Robert Muller, who called his piece prophetically "The Last Tycoon." Spiegel looked like a benign Jewish Buddha and spoke with an attractive accent based a little east of Vienna, said by his friends to be "one of Sam's birthplaces." Spiegel was defending his role as an independent producer and his choice of subjects. Each film had to be a concentration and a dedication. Could a composer write two symphonies at the same time? "The excitement and vocation of my activity is that every time I make a picture I fight all the furies. With each picture I can be ruined." Spiegel defended his making of *Suddenly Last Summer*. There was a lot of identification in cannibalism. "It shows that you can't abuse and devour people without being abused and devoured by them."

Spiegel revealed that there was one film he wanted to make more than his next project, *Lawrence of Arabia*. It was *Don Quixote*, but there was no identification in that. Everybody thought he was Quixote, but lived like Sancho Panza. Spiegel did not say that he did the same, but launched into a presentation of himself as a moralist and a good citizen, concerned with bettering the state of the world. When Muller pointed out that they were riding in a Rolls-Royce with a built-in cigar compartment, Spiegel confessed to owning a good car. As for living on yachts, that was no extravagance. He only chartered them, he said, for he had not yet bought the *Malahne*. And he worked on them, making his films. Yachts merely proved his absolute lack of concern for money. Most people who produced films collected money, but he only wanted pocket-money. Then he spoke the truth. "I need a lot of pocket-money. But all I want is to live generously."

He said he lived alone most of the time. He lived wherever his next picture was. It was difficult to inflict this life on anybody else. He had been married for two years, but he had seen very little of his new wife. His two previous marriages had been very brief. His professional life had always seemed more intriguing than the sacrifices that had to be made in marriage. Spiegel then made a true analysis of and prophecy about himself. "You pay for everything you want by depriving yourself of something you need, and my compensation has been to live a very footloose existence, to live without a harness round my neck. I expect I'll pay for this dearly when I'm older, even older. I fully expect to spend my old age in solitary loneliness." Spiegel left Muller at Heathrow airport, where hordes of Hollywood executives surrounded the great producer. Spiegel gave them all a nod, a wink or a greeting. Then he betrayed his solitude in the crowd that he always needed round him to forget his solitude. "Who are all these people?" he whispered to Muller. "I am getting old. I forget names. I have no idea who they are. People's vanity will not permit them to conceive that you should forget their names."

Nobody forgot the name or the appearance of Spiegel, as he approached the age of sixty. His huge head was set on a heavy squat body and short legs that walked with power and gravity, as though he owned the ground he trod. His face was noble and composed with unutterable wisdom and discretion, his moist eyes lidded with the secrets of his infinite manipulations. His voice was low, his words measured: the ingredients of every sentence were weighed in the balance. His silences were disturbing: they sought entertainment or enlightenment: if he heard neither, he dismissed his petitioner. He cajoled or commanded or judged those he found wanting in giving him what he wanted. He was a loyal friend, a hard master and a terrible enemy. Above all, he had authority and ingenuity, given by God and bitter experience. He was like the hero of the Auden poem, who

> ...Poised between shocking falls on razor-edge
> Has taught himself this balancing subterfuge
> Of the accosting profile, the erect carriage.

Horizon Pictures, based in Zurich and Geneva, bought Spiegel a steam yacht as his floating office, using the profits accruing from the distribution of *The Bridge on the River Kwai*. The *Malahne* had been built in 1937 at Camper & Nicholson's as a luxury steam yacht. It was being refitted at Vosper's for a wealthy Belgian industrialist called Solvay, who named the yacht after his four daughters, but who unfortunately died, giving Spiegel an opportunity to buy the boat. It displaced nearly 500 tons, needed a full crew of twenty-three, and had a paneled dining saloon, a bar and a false fireplace in the main saloon, also six staterooms with a small cabin for Spiegel's stray girls adjoining his master stateroom. An advanced radio room enabled Spiegel to communicate with any place in the world. "If he never took the thing out of the harbor," Bill Graf was told, "it was $150,000 a year." Its full running costs were double that sum. A succession of captains sailed it for Spiegel, who was a Captain Bligh to his crew, a Maecenas to his guests. "His final and most gorgeous blossoming was on his yacht," Talli Wyler said. "He was in control." His black butler, James Jordan, arranged all with a tact that beggared understanding. Money was no object. Anchored in Monte Carlo, Spiegel asked Bill Graf's wife where she would like to go for breakfast. "Portofino," she said. The yacht steamed all night, and breakfast and a swim were had in Portofino before a return to Monte Carlo. On one morning, however, on a trip to Capri with Trevor Howard, the Grafs found themselves abandoned on the island while Spiegel returned to Naples to be shaved at the Excelsior—he never shaved himself—and to fill up the yacht with oil. On that occasion, a huge Neopolitan longshoreman tried to blackmail Spiegel to pay more for his marine fuel. Looming over the producer, he raised a fist and said, "Have you ever seen *On the Waterfront?*"

Just as Spiegel was the catalyst who made the diverse talents on his motion pictures work together, the *Malahne* was the condition of his new success with the European aristocracy. Spiegel's yacht bridged the ditch between celebrity and society. "In the aristocracy of success," S. J. Perelman once wrote, "there are no strangers." The Kennedy family visited the *Malahne*, knowing the value of show-business friends in politics. When Jack Kennedy became president of the United States, it appeared that Spiegel had direct access to the most powerful man in the world. Grace Kelly had already proved how a Hollywood princess could become an actual one. She and her husband, Prince Rainier of Monaco, were frequent guests on the yacht. But the most extraordinary guest was the recluse Greta Garbo. She counted Spiegel as one of her few friends. She was treated as if she were royalty by her usual escort, a Swedish prince who became Count Bernadotte after a later marriage to a commoner. Even Spiegel never kept her waiting. She prized him for his wisdom and his wit and his discretion. The Swedish prince and she would often go on the *Malahne* with the Baron and Baroness Enrico di Portonova, who had been born Gustafson, Garbo's original name. They found Spiegel a generous host and knowledgeable on everything from Italian art history to the politics of Lithuania. He seemed never to sleep, either reading through the nights or playing gin rummy with his friends.

So actresses and princes came together on the *Malahne*. Earl Mountbatten followed and brought along the young Prince of Wales. The decks they trod became magnets for those who valued the association. Spiegel could now request and secure a royal premiere for his next major motion picture, *Lawrence of Arabia*. "He handled his yacht with extraordinary class," Max Youngstein said. "He got class across without irritating you."

While the visitors' book on the *Malahne* was becoming the social register of the Mediterranean world, Spiegel was also setting himself up in state in a penthouse at 475 Park Avenue. The decor was as lavish as the Pope's receiving room for audiences. As Joe Mankiewicz said, "Sam Spiegel is the only Jewish cardinal in New York. That apartment has got to stop being the Vatican." Even the barber's chair he kept in the penthouse looked like a papal throne, while the red hangings and marble tables were intended to be a suitable background for Spiegel's growing collection of Impressionist paintings. He increasingly sought the wise advice of David Somerset, now the Duke of Beaufort, and a director of the Marlborough Galleries. While Somerset provided the expertise, Spiegel was learning as he always did. The basis of his apparent erudition was picking the brains of experts and remembering what they said. He studied through inquiry and conversation, not through textbooks. He was to acquire the works of painters as distinguished as the names on the credits of his films, pictures by Bonnard, Braque, Cézanne (not Kazan), Chagall, Degas, Gauguin, Gris, Kokoschka, Manet, Matisse, Picasso, Pissarro, Renoir, Rouault, Rousseau, Soutine, Utrillo and Vuillard.

Before the penthouse was ready, Max Youngstein saw Spiegel taking some of his paintings off the wall of the Madison Hotel in New York to hide them from his creditors, because he was months in arrears with his hotel bill. He always overspent and lived as if he had millions of dollars in the bank instead of anticipated from the future profits of his films. "He would have top quality and top commercial success. It took a lot of doing. He had an evocative ability to get the best out of people. He was one of the real catalytic men, who went out of his way to be gentle and understanding with people he liked. He would be as tough as nails if somebody did something to outrage him."

As the man in charge of overseas productions in Columbia Pictures, Bill Graf knew of Spiegel's behavior as a producer. Graf approached his job as a partner to the producer, but if he thought Columbia was being ripped off, he replied in kind. He had his differences with Spiegel, particularly over the treatment of the underlings at Horizon Pictures. Spiegel's administrator Gino Cataneo was wizened before his time, afraid of his shadow, carrying "the world on his shoulders all the time, and the world was Sam Spiegel." When Cataneo came shaking into the office for Spiegel to yell at him, Graf would feel compassion and reproach Spiegel, "How can you speak to a man like that?" Once Cataneo brought some Horizon Pictures production checks to Graf to countersign on behalf of Columbia. One of the checks was to Les Ambassadeurs for £28 for a magnum of champagne—the magnum that Spiegel had given to Graf at his birthday party. Graf refused to sign the check, saying, "Same as if I stole the twenty-eight pounds." When he visited Spiegel again, the first thing Spiegel did was to disassociate himself and yell at the shivering Cataneo, "How dare *you* submit that check?" Spiegel had to have his whipping boy, and Cataneo served in that role for him. His other cause for confrontation was the telephone, on which he spent half his life. His rows over the black instrument were legendary. He seemed to need at least two quarrels a day to make himself function at his best.

Yet Spiegel was the best producer in Europe, the most creative producer, and the most discriminating. And he was about to embark on his greatest production of all, when he would not count the cost or the effort, only the power and the glory.

CHAPTER TEN

Lawrence of Arabia

Justice Has Triumphed
UNIVERSAL'S LAWYERS
Appeal Immediately
CARL LAEMMLE

Spiegel could never admit to doing wrong. "One observation I make," Graf said over an incident on their next production together, *Lawrence of Arabia*, "and it covers our entire industry from my experience—men who are in power are just afraid to tell the truth." The incident concerned the hiring of a blue-eyed French actor, Christian Marquand, who went out to Jordan, began filming, was unable to speak English well enough to satisfy David Lean and had to be replaced. He was only told, however, that he would be returning to France during a break in the shooting. Graf still had the contact lenses for making Marquand's blue eyes brown, so he asked Spiegel why he would not tell the actor the truth. Spiegel only shrugged and had the actor's clothes and Arabic rugs sent after him. The truth was, as Graf knew, that Omar Sharif might give an even worse performance, leading to the recall of the unfortunate Frenchman. The only truth in the making of a film is in making a good end product. Truth is not a factor in how a film is made.

Spiegel needed all his diplomatic skills to develop *Lawrence of Arabia*. By a stroke of intuition, he had engaged as his right-hand man Anthony Nutting, who had been the British Minister of State for Foreign Affairs, before being forced to resign over the Suez Crisis. Nutting was an Arabist, writing a book on T. E. Lawrence, and had been engaged by Spiegel after the New York premiere of *The Bridge on the River Kwai*. Now married to an international model, Ann Gunning, Anthony Nutting praised Spiegel for his film, saying that it was the first time he had been conscious of what direction really was and how tension was built up by it. He was hired by Spiegel as his "Oriental Counsellor" with an impossible mission, to make the Jewish producer acceptable in Arabic countries that had an economic boycott of Israel. Nutting claimed that these matters were never even raised by his friend, the king of Jordan, but this omission had something to do with his diplomatic skills. "You're the only person who can persuade the king of Jordan," the executive Harry Koenitz said, "that Sam Spiegel isn't Jewish." Nutting did more, getting the king's blessing on the film without submitting a final script, although some of the leading characters were the king's uncles and grandfather, the founders of the dynasty.

It had been hard enough to secure the rights to film *Lawrence of Arabia*. Alexander Korda had long wanted to make a feature on the subject himself. So had the Rank Organisation, which owned the rights to film Lawrence's autobiography, *The Seven Pillars of Wisdom*. Many treatments had been made for screenplays, many actors considered for the leading role—Robert Donat, Leslie Howard, Laurence Olivier, Alec Guinness and Dirk Bogarde. In fact, when Spiegel acquired the rights to Lawrence's autobiography, Dirk Bogarde had been set to play Lawrence in a blond wig for a Rank version, scripted by Terence Rattigan, to be shot in Iraq on a budget of half a million pounds. He had never wanted a part so much, but a few weeks before shooting was due to begin, the project was canceled and the rights sold for a mere £20,000 to Spiegel. "It was my bitterest disappointment," Bogarde said. Alec Guinness played Lawrence in the stage version of the Rattigan screenplay, called *Ross*, while Spiegel wanted Marlon Brando to act the lead in his film. Another film based on *Ross* to star Laurence Harvey also collapsed. Spiegel bought up the rights of other biographies on Lawrence, including four books by the poet Robert Graves, and reckoned that he had eliminated any rival version. His opponents had been spiegeled, but not impoverished. As one of the paid biographers said to Spiegel, "I am glad that my hands are clean, but not empty."

Lawrence of Arabia had not been the first choice as a subject for the next Spiegel production with David Lean. "Our first idea was to make a film," Lean said, "of the life and death of Mahatma Gandhi." They had approached the project cautiously, because it was presumptuous to film the life of a man believed to be a saint. They abandoned the project, later to be filmed by Sir Richard Attenborough, with relief and disappointment. "To dramatize we must simplify. To simplify we must leave something out." It was too much of a responsibility to decide what to leave out of Gandhi's life.

Lawrence's life, however, was easier to simplify, although not his complex character. Other than his dramatic death on a motorcycle, the chief events of his life in Arabia took place in two years at the end of the First World War. The problem was to find a screenwriter able to explore so devious and formidable a personality, yet to convey in spare dialogue the quality and resonance of Lawrence's own descriptions of the campaign and himself. At first, Spiegel turned again to Michael Wilson, who spent a year with him on the *Malahne* working on the script. But a screenplay satisfactory to Lean and Spiegel could not be found because of what the producer called "natural frictions." It lacked what Lawrence's own work, *The Seven Pillars of Wisdom*, had lacked, "that blue thread of continuity every picture must have." In despair, Spiegel turned to Eddie Chodorov, now forgiven for his correct advice to Lynn Baggett and working for Horizon Pictures as a general adviser, screenwriter and production executive. Chodorov said that he could not do the script, which needed a British writer. He took Spiegel to see Robert Bolt's current success in the theater, *A Man for All Seasons*. The play dealt with the relationship of Sir Thomas More with King Henry VIII, who finally had him executed for failing to justify the royal actions.

Spiegel originally wanted Bolt only to rewrite the dialogue in the Wilson script, but Bolt insisted on writing his own version of Lawrence's character. They began work on the day before Christmas of 1960, and Bolt finished eighteen months later. He wanted to write something more than a camel opera. As David Lean said, the script was essentially Bolt's conception of Lawrence, who had written about his own "madness" and tendencies to sadism and masochism. "That's an idea, a theme—" Spiegel said later, "how easily a man can be a demon and a prophet at the same time, a Hitler and Zarathustra."

In his screenplay of *Lawrence of Arabia*, Bolt tried to match his subject in "a bold and beautiful verbal architecture." He had not realised that one and a half gruelling years would be taken from his life to build the blocks. Spiegel and Lean, he complained, had taken him over body and soul. They were always ripping the script apart and examining it and demanding more and more rewriting. "It was all like a rugby scramble really." He had to go to Jordan on reconnaissance trips and during shooting. He thought the filming was the biggest job since the building of the Pyramids, where egomaniacal monsters clashed continuously and wasted more energy than dinosaurs while pouring rivers of money into the sand. He was actively involved in the Campaign for Nuclear Disarmament and found himself sentenced to a month's imprisonment for defying a magistrate and refusing to recant, as Sir Thomas More had refused.

Spiegel would not allow his screenwriter to be confined to jail unable to write. The prison governor had refused to allow Bolt pen and paper. Spiegel sent telegrams to Bolt insisting that he recant and be released. Otherwise, the whole film production would stop, the four million pounds of its budget would be lost. Bolt refused to give way. Spiegel drove down to the jail in Staffordshire. He used threats and cajolery to change Bolt's mind. Hundreds of jobs, millions of pounds depended on the writer compromising with his conscience and completing the words for *Lawrence of Arabia*. Bolt believed him while not believing him. "Bob baby," Spiegel would say, tears pouring down his face, "would I do a thing to you like that? Would I not tell you the truth? This is on my heart." If Bolt still hesitated, "then Spiegel would find a little corridor behind me." That corridor led to the prison governor's office, where Bolt signed his recantation. Spiegel had been more successful than King Henry VIII with Sir Thomas More. He had changed his writer's sense of conviction without having him executed. "I have never forgiven him," Bolt still says, "for getting me out of prison."

In point of fact, Bolt had an immediate, but unintentional, revenge. That evening, Anthony Nutting telephoned Spiegel and said, "I hear you have been in jail." There was a silence and Spiegel banged down the receiver. Nutting did not understand Spiegel's reaction and asked David Lean the reason why. "Oh God, you didn't say that," Lean answered. "Sam was."

The casting for the film went through its various permutations. Marlon Brando was working with Sir Carol Reed on another version of *Mutiny on the Bounty*, and the schedule was being extended. Spiegel now believed that Brando had become a different kind of actor—tortured and difficult to work with. David Lean also feared that the actor might impose his style and character on the part. He did not want to make a Brando of Arabia. Anthony Perkins was also considered, but again there were fears of a Psycho of Arabia. Alec Guinness was too old to play Lawrence on film, and Lean no longer wanted to work with him after the bruising confrontations on their previous film. Spiegel said that Guinness would have been offered the part if he had been fifteen years younger, but privately assured Lean that Guinness would not be given a role in the film.

The young Albert Finney was the next choice to play Lawrence after his success in *The Entertainer* and *Saturday Night and Sunday Morning*. One hundred thousand pounds were spent on a screen test of him. He impressed Spiegel, but not Lean, who thought Finney had too many ideas and wanted to direct the picture. In the event, Finney did not want to sign a five-year contract with Spiegel for a fee of £250,000. His freedom as an artist was more important to him. His friends could tell him that he might be led like a horse to water, but even Spiegel could not make him drink. Yet he did not believe them and insisted on liberty more than money. "There'll be others," he said. "Plenty of people have been ruined by Hollywood. I want to be an actor, not a marketable property like a detergent."

So Spiegel went again to Peter O'Toole, much against the grain after the debacle of the screen test for *Suddenly Last Summer*. Katharine Hepburn had insisted to Spiegel that O'Toole was the finest young actor in London, and now he was playing Shylock superbly in *The Merchant of Venice* for Peter Hall and for the Royal Shakespeare Company, which sued to keep its star. O'Toole was not enamoured of Stratford, which he called Okefenokee-on-Avon, a swamp and a culture drome. Spiegel insisted that O'Toole should endure another stringent film test in full Arab costume. This time O'Toole held his tongue until Spiegel did finally offer him the role of Lawrence. Only then did O'Toole ask, "Is it a speaking part?"

The other speaking parts were assigned. After Cary Grant and Laurence Olivier had turned down General Allenby, the part went to Jack Hawkins. When Kirk Douglas was not available as the American reporter, Arthur Kennedy took the role. Anthony Quinn was chosen to play Auda Abu Tayi with a false nose; José Ferrer the sadistic Turkish bey; Claude Rains the devious British diplomat; and finally Alec Guinness was to appear as Prince Feisal. Shooting had already begun when Spiegel announced to Lean that Guinness was playing in the film despite quarrels during the shooting of *The Bridge on the River Kwai*. Lean immediately stopped work and announced he was leaving the picture. According to legend, Spiegel fell to the ground, the apparent victim of a heart attack. Rushed away to the hospital, he was put in an oxygen tent. The stricken Lean visited him, offering to give Spiegel anything he wanted, anything, if it would help him to recover. Spiegel immediately revived and smiled and said, "You're so nice. So we cast Alec Guinness."

The part of the Arab hero Sheikh Ali, caused another succession of problems. Horst Buchholz was the first choice and Christian Marquand the second, but when the French actor showed little command of English, someone else had to be found. Spiegel and Mike Frankovich went to Cairo to sign an Egyptian actress for the part of an Arabian princess, only to sign up her husband instead, Omar Sharif. He played the part for only $40,000 and accepted a seven-picture deal that held him on low pay through many later successes like *Funny Girl* in spite of attempts by his agents to tear up the contract. It was David Lean who taught him to act, curbing his Middle Eastern temperament and saying, "He who can do the most can do the least." In Cairo to interview Sharif, Spiegel showed a terror of being poisoned because he was Jewish, even though Anthony Nutting had filled in his religion on the visa application as Church of England. So fearful of poisoning was Spiegel that he even boiled the water for brushing his teeth.

Fear of another kind was seen by Robert Bolt when staying with Spiegel on the *Malahne* moored off Aqaba. While flying there, Bolt had looked down from the airplane at the minuscule boat on the Red Sea and said, "What do you suppose the Arabs think when they see your yacht?" Spiegel had answered, "I expect they say those lousy Jews are everywhere." But that night, Bolt was sleeping in the large saloon of the yacht with Spiegel nearby. He woke a little before his producer and watched Spiegel's face as the other man woke to the working day. "He had forgotten I was there. His face was a mask of despair. Then he composed it and smiled and said, 'Hello.' But you see, he would never give in."

Most of Spiegel's fears lay in his dealings with the Jordanian army and its officers, which had fought against Israel. Anthony Nutting proved worth his weight in sovereigns. In the negotiations for the use of the Jordanian army, Nutting had the asking price reduced from one million pounds to one hundred and fifty thousand. Spiegel arrived late at the meeting, and Nutting had the door locked on him in case he would spoil the agreement. But when Spiegel heard of the huge saving, he upgraded Nutting's term of endearment from "baby" to "sweetheart." It was a sweetheart deal.

Nutting also suggested the locations in the Empty Quarter—the red dunes and cliffs of Wadi Rumm and Jebel Tubeiq near the Saudi Arabian frontier, two hundred and fifty miles east of the port of Aqaba where the *Malahne* was moored. When David Lean had asked Nutting why he found the desert so attractive, Nutting had said it was because it was so clean. Driving out to visit the unit camp in a sandstorm, Nutting met a smiling Lean caked in red dust. "All you said about the desert was an understatement," Lean said. "It's a very clean place." He became almost mystical. He would rise in the night before each day's shooting and sit staring at the sunrise over the dunes so that the actors and technicians would find him brooding there first of all. Because of the extreme heat, shooting could only take place in the early morning and the evening. At midday, only armies of sweepers with palm leaves moved over the sand, brushing away the footprints on the dunes that showed anyone had been to the Empty Quarter before.

Through the good offices of Nutting, Spiegel even became quite friendly with the king of Jordan, who spent two days aboard the *Malahne*, drinking champagne and smoking Monte Cristo cigars, Number Two. In return, he asked Spiegel and Lean and certain of the actors and the crew to come to dinner in the palace at Amman. Spiegel gave everybody a lecture on etiquette. With Israel over the border and the West Bank of the River Jordan in dispute, no religion or politics were to be discussed. To his horror at the dinner, Spiegel heard a member of the crew asking the king, "What is Ramadan?" As the king tried patiently to explain, Spiegel bellowed down the table, "You know exactly what it is—it's just like our Lent." The king flew his own Hawker Hunter fighter and repeatedly buzzed the production office in Aqaba. "Oh, there goes Flash," the staff would say, not understanding the reason for the royal attention until one of the bilingual secretaries became the king's next wife.

While making *Lawrence of Arabia*, Spiegel gave various interviews. One of them, by James Fixx, was called "The Spiegel Touch" and recognized that Spiegel was the last of the great creative producers, worthy to stand after Sam Goldwyn and Thalberg and Selznick. He had an enormous confidence in his own ability to get things done, the performance to justify the confidence, and a consistent serendipity that was the envy and despair of lesser men. "Spiegel, like T. E. Lawrence, is a baffling complex person. His cultured Viennese accent, with its overtones of London and Park Avenue, can at one moment convey a meltingly persuasive charm, and at the next dismiss an idea or person with one crisp word. He can be as guileless as a child or, when it suits his purposes, his associates say, he can plot with the patience and strategic cunning of a grand master at chess. But above all, he knows how to get his way."

Get his way he did on *Lawrence of Arabia*. The logistics were awesome. Jebel Tubeiq had no water, had been deserted since the seventh century, and consisted of a ruined monastery and brilliant red sand dunes. The actors and crew had to be quartered in Nissen huts: only the stars had trailers and air conditioning. Water was trucked in from a hundred and fifty miles away, food flown in from Britain. Temperatures reached one hundred and thirty degrees. The thermometers had to be cooled to prevent them from exploding by recording the true temperatures. Four thousand Bedouins and hundreds of camels congregated there and had to be fed. The beasts were valued more highly than the humans; a camel's wages were four pounds a month, a Bedouin's one pound. The meticulous Lean took three months of preparation to begin shooting, then a year to film in the Jordanian desert at a cost of £50,000 a week. He seemed never to want to leave for the other locations in Spain and Morocco. "Making a film does get to be a drug for me," he later admitted. "Once started, it's hard for me to stop."

Spiegel had to drag Lean away from the dunes. "When the time came to go he was almost tearful," Spiegel said. But the producer could not afford any more time or money. Columbia Pictures would not tolerate further extravagance. Spiegel had lured Columbia into the project initially by submitting an artificially low budget, which grew to £2,800,000. Lean's love affair with the desert increased the budget by one and a half million pounds, to £4,300,000. This was too much, and Columbia shared Spiegel's fear that another war might break out between Israel and its Arab neighbors and stop the shooting of the film. It was not that Spiegel or Lean tried to waste money, Mike Frankovich said, but neither one of them tried to save money. Spiegel was put on the defensive and made a famous remark: 'I never use a thousand camels when only a couple of hundred will do."

The actual cities of Aqaba and Cairo, Damascus and Jerusalem could not be used as they looked too modern. They had to be reproduced in Almeira and Seville in Spain, as did the old Hejaz Railway. In Seville itself, the Casa Paladuz, said to be a copy of Pontius Pilate's palace in Jerusalem, was lent by the Duchess of Medina-Celli to Spiegel as a background for *Lawrence of Arabia*. As usual, the film technicians were no connoisseurs of antiquity. For them, the four statues in the four corners of the palace courtyard were obstacles in the race to hitch up electrical cables. On one occasion, a cable became wrapped round a Roman statue and was tugged violently. A marble arm fell off and broke in three pieces. That afternoon, the duchess arrived to watch the shooting with Peter O'Toole and Jack Hawkins. Both the actors apologized for the mishap to the marble statue. The duchess agreed that it was a pity, but it could be repaired. "And, after all, it *was* only Roman." She showed a nice disregard for antiquity and history, about which Spiegel and his art director, John Box, were so meticulous.

The final massacre sequence was to be filmed in a Moroccan town, south of the Atlas mountains, called Ouarzazate, where French legionnaires were once sent for punishment in the intense heat. Spiegel worried that the film would never end—it seemed that it would run for four hours—and that his star O'Toole might not last the course. He forbade O'Toole to fly for fear of risking his life. "Spiegel treats me as if I were Rin-Tin-Tin," O'Toole complained, "instead of a working actor." He did nearly die when thrown off his camel during a cavalry charge and shot in the right eye with pellets from an effects gun. But professional that he was, he was back on the set next day. He also nearly died when the towing-bar snapped in his final motorcycle sequence. He thought that Lawrence himself, who had died on a motorcycle, was teasing him from heaven. But Spiegel would not have been amused.

When told that the shooting could not go on forever, David Lean had said, "Why not?" Through his new royal connections, Spiegel found a brilliant device to make his director come to a halt. He told Lean that *Lawrence of Arabia* had been scheduled for the Royal Film Performance in front of the Queen on December 10, 1962. Would Lean disappoint Her Majesty? Lean capitulated and said it was a wrap. O'Toole thought it was a master stroke, fixing the premiere date and inviting the Queen before shooting had ended. They had begun to forget they were making a film. "After two years it had become a way of life—so Sam nailed us with a date and that was that." Lean moved into the cutting room, telling Nutting, "My film is not what I leave in, but what I leave on the cutting room floor." Spiegel was battling to get the film they wanted. The executives of Columbia Pictures were horrified that the final cut ran for three hours and forty minutes: it meant that they would lose a showing a day on release. But Spiegel fought them and fought them again and won, by intransigence and cunning. He was like Lawrence in the film, slowly putting out a burning match with his fingers. When asked what was the trick to make it not hurt, Lawrence replied, "Of course it hurts. The trick is not minding that it hurts."

The love-hate relationship between Spiegel and Lean broke down with the ending of the film. Mike Frankovich had been the arbiter between them, but even his diplomacy could not heal the final rift. Both men had to dominate. As Ben Hecht once said, there were two Caesars and only one Alp. In Robert Bolt's opinion, Spiegel lacked only one thing to become a very great producer—and Lean lacked it as a director. Neither was generous by nature. Both were always trying to see who could get the better of the other. "Spiegel had great generosity," Bolt said, "but not generosity of spirit. He had to buy you."

Lean now wanted to become a Spiegel and always work on a large scale. "You know, bloody millionaire stuff," he said. He had a Swiss-based company with Spiegel, but he sold his share later to his partner and to Columbia. He declared that he wanted to go to the Far East for his next picture—"the farthest way to get from Sam Spiegel." Once more, as with John Huston, Spiegel would lose the fine director he needed to make his best pictures for him. But he would never lose control of the pictures that they had made together.

Lawrence of Arabia repeated the success of *The Bridge on the River Kwai*. Only in Hollywood did Spiegel require his skill at saving his reputation. Peter O'Toole had insisted that Omar Sharif should also be flown in for the premiere. The evening before, the two actors went to see Lenny Bruce perform, were arrested by the neighborhood drugs squad and incarcerated. Spiegel was telephoned and arrived in the jail flanked by six lawyers. They went into a secret conference with the police. Sharif and O'Toole were released, but O'Toole would not leave without Lenny Bruce. Eventually all three were turned loose, and the Hollywood police were spiegeled. "The story never hit the papers," Sharif commented, "but it must have cost Sam Spiegel an arm and a leg."

Lawrence of Arabia won eight Oscars and Spiegel himself won a third Oscar for his work as producer. He was accepted by the Hollywood Academy as well as by European society. He had triumphed over the box office and the critics and, unforgivably, abroad. But he even sought to make a local kind of peace, telling *Variety* that American technicians had unrivaled superiority and working conditions in Hollywood were much more peaceful. There was no doubt that he would return. Even so, the subject of a film might demand that it should be shot on foreign shores. Spiegel had heard of the Hollywood joker saying, "If you like Palm Springs, you'd love Lawrence." But the point was that *Lawrence of Arabia* was a great picture largely because it was obviously not made in Palm Springs.

Spiegel's invention of a respectable past was completed by the time he issued his brief autobiography for publicity purposes before the opening of *Lawrence of Arabia*. He claimed to have been born in Austria, not in Poland, which was not mentioned at all. Nor was Palestine. He asserted that his first marriage was with a young American girl, whom he divorced before the birth of his daughter, now married and living in Philadelphia.

He implied that he lived in Austria until he came to America in 1927, after specializing in the study of economics, dramatic literature and languages at the University of Vienna. He had not been a cotton broker when he first visited America, but had been invited to present a series of lectures on European drama for an extension course at Berkeley. It was there that the MGM producer Paul Bern had found him, while on a location trip to see the university's Greek Theater. Bern had been so impressed with Spiegel's erudition that he had hired him as his adviser on foreign literature, with authority to buy properties in French, German, Spanish and Italian. Only when there was friction with Bern did Spiegel move on to work as a translator for Carl Laemmle at Universal Pictures, before being sent to Berlin as Universal's man there. Spiegel's father was presented as a scholar and a literary man, who only worked as a wholesale tobacconist to keep his family, and who died in the 1930s. Spiegel's mother had encouraged her younger son's bent for scholarly pursuits to follow in the steps of his elder brother, Shalom, who had become a professor at the University of Vienna and the youngest member of its faculty.

In all, a most distinguished past, but distinguished as much for its omissions as its veracities. When *Time* magazine featured Spiegel, it called him as arbitrary about his background as he used to be about his name, S. P. Eagle. Yet its description of the producer on ceremony was splendid. "The gait was unhurried, the paunch impressive as a Roman emperor's, the head massive as a Percheron's. Producer Sam Spiegel, to the strains of the theme music from *Lawrence of Arabia*, was advancing down the side of the Santa Monica Civic Auditorium to accept the Academy Award for Best Picture of the Year." When he later won the Irving G. Thalberg Award for contributions to motion pictures and joined the illustrious names of Zanuck, Selznick, Disney and Goldwyn, he laid to rest forever the old canard of the 1940s: "Spiegel can do anything except make a picture."

One last controversy marred the triumph of *Lawrence of Arabia*. The hero's brother, a professor and archaeologist, denounced the film as false. "They have used a psychological recipe," he declared. "Take an ounce of narcissism, a pound of exhibitionism, a pint of sadism, a gallon of blood-lust and a sprinkle of other aberrations and stir well." Robert Bolt refuted these charges, particularly the accusation that his own pacifism had led him to portray Lawrence as a maniac ready to sacrifice innocent people. But Spiegel as always had the last word, knowing that the Lawrence depicted on the film would become mightier than the Lawrence of his own pen. He had rescued Lawrence from Victorian cleanliness and the false footprints he had planted about himself. Life should imitate art, not the other way round. There had never been any question of filming *The Seven Pillars of Wisdom*, but of seeking some of the truths behind a man who still remained exceptional. "We did not try to solve the legend of Lawrence of Arabia, we tried to perpetuate it."

CHAPTER ELEVEN

When He Stopped Listening

He who eats my bread sings my song.

HARRY COHN

"The jig was up with Sam Spiegel," Eddie Chodorov said, "when he stopped listening." He stopped listening when he had completed *Lawrence of Arabia* and had quarreled with David Lean. He was never to work again with so great a director nor to recreate the necessary tension in making the films he wanted to make. He now needed to dictate, and few dared to oppose him. Chodorov and other close associates were to leave him because he would no longer listen to them. "Spiegelitis," so Chodorov diagnosed the producer's condition, "a disease of calling all the terms, a hundred and two percent fever."

One of Spiegel's golden Oscars still stands in the Columbia Pictures office of Leo Jaffe, who has his own citation for fifty years of dedicated service and leadership of the company. He used to bargain with Spiegel over film financing and percentages, he would fight Spiegel on shooting over schedule and the final cut, but he ended as the arbiter in any dispute between Spiegel and his directors or Columbia. Although none of the films that Spiegel made after *Lawrence of Arabia* ever repeated its success, most of them broke even eventually, while the profits from three blockbusters still came rolling in as regularly as the tides. There was no written agreement or even a memorandum between Spiegel and Columbia Pictures, only shared profits. When Spiegel was asked why he did not shop around, he observed. "The devil I know is better than the devils I don't know."

Jaffe knew Spiegel to be the loneliest of men, although surrounded by hordes of friends and acquaintances. He could confide in nobody. He could only play the man of taste and culture, generosity and sympathy, which he now appeared to be and had not always been. Yet after many years, appearances become reality. Acquired characteristics develop into true character. So it was with Spiegel in the 1960s. His giving became legendary, now that he could afford it. He went to extreme lengths to arrange for

David Selznick to produce another picture on his own terms. It was the kind of thing, Selznick's first wife Irene wrote, that Selznick would have been likely to do, but not something he would have expected from colleagues. "Sam Spiegel gave himself to you," Evelyn Keyes recalled, "or he did not. He was available for your troubles twenty-four hours. That is, if you were pretty. I'm not sure that was true if you weren't—or weren't talented."

One characteristic that Spiegel could not change was his compulsion to have young women around him. He had to prove his ageless youth and his success through his serials of girls. His mania led to rifts with his professional companions. The director Fred Zinnemann finally broke with him after yet another production meeting was interrupted by endless calls from Spiegel to his young women. "It was a game of dominance," Zinnemann said. Spiegel had to show virility and mastery to the celebrities who were his guests and chose to ignore the passing youth parade.

While cruising on the *Malahne*, Spiegel would find girls at every port and take them to the next port, where they were replaced or exchanged. Their numbers were legion, their names a guide to Europe and an alphabet—Ann, Brigid, Charlotte, Dagmar, Eugenie, Francesca, Gretchen, Heather. . . . He would invite them aboard, when he saw them paddling around his yacht in their little boats and pedalos, waiting to be picked up. Their boyfriends would be left behind. He offered Lady Keith, previously married to the director Howard Hawks and the Broadway producer Leland Hayward, the exclusive use of the *Malahne*, then moored in Barcelona, because she was depressed during a divorce. When she arrived to take possession, she found Spiegel already there and a couple of German girls, who were more interested in each other than in Spiegel. But they were dropped off in the South of France and more taken aboard.

Young girls were always a part of Spiegel's life, He collected them like a pasha. They were the producer's prerogative. There had been a bevy of them upstairs at his house on Crescent Drive when he was giving his parties. Like Charles Chaplin before him and Roman Polanski after him he had trouble from his liaisons with girls below the age of consent, but he managed to settle the legal problems. He did not have to leave Hollywood because of them. He had four or five girls in tow in London, when he was setting up the financial deal on *The African Queen* with the Woolf brothers. His associates on the film had found him generous with the girls' company. He was never jealous or exclusive about those who came and went by day and night. The apartment in Grosvenor Square, which he had taken for the duration of the film and was to keep, had two entrances. There always seemed to be a girl leaving by the back as another entered the front. Spiegel rose late. He never reached a morning production meeting on time, finally irritating John Woolf beyond endurance. "We could not always wait for Sam," Woolf said. "But he was such a charming and cultivated man."

Lord Bernstein called Spiegel's compulsion over girls a disease of possession. Spiegel had to have too much of what he had never had as a young man. His appetite for girls and rich possessions could never be satisfied. He was unlike Charles Chaplin, who once confessed to Lord Bernstein, "All those young women—I was only looking for one woman, and I found Oona," his last wife. Spiegel never found his one woman nor his ultimate possession.

Bernstein did not ever think that Spiegel's natural good taste applied to his yacht, the *Malahne*, which was the vulgar dream boat of the poor boy from Poland. Although it had more style than the yachts of the *nouveau riche* Docker and Onassis, it was still ostentatious and overstated. For those on board, the *Malahne* was both paradise and the inferno. The guests were fed and wined to death and every attention lavished upon them; but if they tried to go ashore or stop the boat for a swim, it was hell at sea. Spiegel was in command, and even his captains knew it. They appeared and vanished so frequently from the bridge that they seemed as easily replaceable as actors between films. "Always some honky-tonk captain," one regular guest said, "although one was really from the Royal Navy." Once, docking at Saint-Tropez, the *Malahne* took all the masts off the next yacht. But if captains could come and captains could go, it seemed that Spiegel would go on forever. He certainly believed that he would never die. It would create a gap in nature, the removal of an elemental force. "I believe in mortality," Spiegel once said, "but not in inflicting it upon myself."

The visitors' book on the *Malahne* was a roll call of film stars and executives, aristocrats and celebrities, politicians and writers. Yet all of them had their due dates and times of invitation. Spiegel's worlds were not allowed to mix. He remained the ringmaster of the various cages and compartments in which he tried to keep his innumerable friends. If Leo Jaffe or Mike Frankovich or Albert Broccoli came on board, they would meet the William Wylers or the Anatole Litvaks or the George Stevenses, who were lent the *Malahne* for their honeymoon. They would be the guests on the yacht when it was anchored off Cannes for the annual film festival, which Spiegel bestrode like a marine colossus. If Jean Kennedy Smith or Pat Kennedy Lawford came with their husbands, they would meet other film actors or European politicians and aristocracy. Only film stars were universal on the *Malahne*, for everybody wanted to meet them—Brigitte Bardot and Sophia Loren, Warren Beatty and Julie Christie, William Holden and Kirk Douglas. Burt Lancaster was aboard with Noël Coward, who found the ship the acme of luxury, but chiefly enjoyed a piss-up with its crew in Ville-franche, asking himself, "Why is it that all English seamen have such unfailing good manners?" But only Coward was allowed to meet the artist Graham Sutherland and the banker Evelyn Baring when they came to visit. And when Henry Kissinger arrived and the talk was of world politics, the other guests would be Edward Heath, the British prime minister, or President Kennedy's advisers such as the historian Arthur Schlesinger, or the Rothschilds or Margot Fonteyn with her diplomat husband. In his orchestration of his guests from various walks of life, Spiegel shared Kissinger's gift, his *Fingerspitzengefühl*, his instinctive feel for a situation. He lent the *Malahne* to Steve and Jean Kennedy Smith the week after Bobby Kennedy was killed, so that they could get away from it all.

Spiegel's new acquaintances rose to the steps of palaces. Some Italian and French aristocrats still considered him an *arrevista*, a cold fish interested in them only for their titles and beauty: on a visit with Spiegel to the Agnellis, Robert Bolt saw his producer performing like a schoolboy because he was so excited by the grand company. Yet many other aristocrats, such as Baron Enrico di Portonova, found Spiegel a natural gentleman, learned and erudite, with the gift of making friends with all the world. Spiegel's contacts reached as high as Buckingham Palace. He became known to Prince Philip through Les Ambassadeurs, the London club run by a gigantic fellow Pole, Johnny Mills, who had no respect for yachts because all who owned them insisted on showing him pictures of them. But it did result in an invitation that solved Spiegel's status with his snobbish office manager in London, Norman Spencer, who complained that Spiegel was not the sort of fellow one could invite to one's club. "That's terrible," Eddie Chodorov replied, "because today he's having lunch with the Queen."

Power and the pursuit of perfection were making Spiegel an autocrat, even if a man of contradictions. He gratified all the opposite desires in himself as instantly as possible. To Irene Selznick, he was simultaneously the arrogant master and the wheeler-dealer, the sympathetic friend and the fixer of troubles. Control was all. He had to be the total producer. And on the *Malahne*, he could control and produce all. In his creased and tailored white shorts, with his large bare stomach aloft and his walkie-talkie in his hand, Spiegel was always in command, ashore or afloat. The mate of the yacht, dressed in immaculate whites, would stand at attention as the duty boat ferried the guests from ship to shore at Spiegel's discretion. On the only occasion that a dog was allowed on board because Spiegel desired its owner, a German actress, the creature was sent ashore with an honor guard twice a day—in William Wyler's words—on Operation Pipi. The guests fared little better. "At times," Talli Wyler said, "if I didn't get off the yacht, I'd have gone crazy." Aboard, it seemed impossible to leave without Spiegel's permission. Once when new guests went up the gangplank at Monte Carlo, they were met by a girl in a large-brimmed hat, who said softly to each of them, "Help!" but did not get off the boat. And when Robert Bolt admired the suntan on another involuntary guest on the *Malahne*, saying what a lovely color she was, he was surprised to see the beautiful woman's eyes fill with tears. "Yes," she said, "it is the color of idleness."

Spiegel was never idle. Even his hospitality was another weapon in his armory. Before he had become wealthy, he had used token generosity as a negotiating tool. When Evelyn Keyes's agent, Douglas Whitney, was settling her fee for performing in *The Prowler*, Spiegel had bought him smoked salmon and scrambled eggs for lunch in Lucey's. But every time Whitney had tried to get more money for his client, Spiegel would take his plate away and return it only when the price was right. "Don't bargain," Spiegel had said, "if you're eating my food."

Those who were taking his bread, particularly as screenwriters, found it impossible to bargain with his point of view on a script. He had begun to develop many important films, three of which ended in such disagreements on the screenplay that they were made by other hands. The first was William Golding's classic novel, *The Lord of the Flies*, which Peter Brook wanted to adapt and direct. After working through seven draft screenplays with Spiegel, Brook ended with one that was not the picture that he was going to make. Yet they had reached a point where Brook had to accept it and trust to the hope that on an unknown island, where the film was set, he might be able to cheat another script on the spot. Finally, he broke with Spiegel and bought the rights to make the film himself, with Spiegel overcharging him in a screaming match between the deep and shallow ends of a swimming pool in the South of France. The final screenplay, however, had its uses, to show financiers, actors and technicians. Although it would have nothing to do with the finished picture, Brook was then able "to go ahead and make the film actually *without a script.*"

Such a method of making a movie was anathema to Spiegel. The director had to shoot the script as constructed. That was what all the years of rewriting were about, before shooting started. He had the same problems with François Truffaut on the Ray Bradbury project, *Fahrenheit 451*, which Truffaut finally shot his own way with other financing. And on *The Country Girls*, a piece by Edna O'Brien, Spiegel assigned Eddie Chodorov to adapt it for the screen, when Chodorov knew no more of Eire than the occasional rendition of "When Irish Eyes Are Smiling" by a tenor in an American bar. Chodorov failed at the adaption and begged Spiegel to send for the playwright Brendan Behan. Behan duly appeared at the airport with a little old lady in black, whom he introduced with the words, "Boys, I want you to meet my effing mother." Offered in Spiegel's office an advance of $15,000 against $75,000 to do the script, Behan said he would settle for three hundred dollars on the table to pay for his bar bills in London. Spiegel was frightened by such Irish immediacy, dropped Behan and gave up the project. He was like Sam Goldwyn, who would rather deal with a smart idiot than a stupid genius.

Two other projects that aborted at the time because of Spiegel's efforts to control the screenplays were Harold Pinter's script of *The Accident*, eventually filmed by Joseph Losey, and *The Curious Gentlemen*, an Edwardian comedy of manners to be written by the stars of the fashionable revue *Beyond the Fringe*, Peter Cook and Dudley Moore and Alan Bennett, and to be directed by Jonathan Miller. On the other hand, two other projects with Columbia Pictures were being finalized. By 1965, Spiegel's five films produced for them had grossed $100,000,000 in worldwide rentals, *Lawrence of Arabia* earning $35,000,000, *On the Waterfront* $30,000,000, and *The Bridge on the River Kwai* $27,000,000. Spiegel agreed with Columbia to make his first Hollywood picture in a decade, *The Chase*, and a European picture, *The Night of the Generals*. Both were intended to be on the scale of his previous major successes.

Spiegel considered himself an elder statesman of the cinema. Pope Paul VI held a private audience with him to discuss the problems of making motion pictures. The Pope supported a self-regulatory mechanism for censoring films, and Spiegel declared himself greatly moved by His Holiness's interest and concern. O'Toole later asserted that Spiegel always traveled on a Vatican passport, but that was an exaggeration.

Spiegel made an attempt to acquire a major distributor of British films, British Lion, but failed in the bid. He agreed to produce six television films for $1,000,000 donated by Xerox to publicize the peace-keeping activities of the United Nations, but the first one on Kashmir foundered in the usual difficulties over a script. Fred Zinnemann walked out of the project, never to return.

When Spiegel finally arrived back in Hollywood to begin making *The Chase*, he lectured his peers about their collective responsibility in producing pictures. They had the opportunity to reach one-third of humanity and show what the American image of life was. For the world did not see America in terms of events there, but in terms of movies. Fifty years on, men would say of the Americans, "Those morons had no idea what power they had or how to utilize it!" It was criminal that Hollywood moviemakers saw nothing in the movies but sensationalism, sex and Lord knew what else. Spiegel felt strongly that the motion picture was the visual language of the future.

He had increasing trouble with the visual language of his next films. Many professional movie-makers believed that a Spiegel film was only as good as its director and even its writers. All the films that Spiegel produced after *Lawrence of Arabia* seemed to prove this point. Spiegel was never again to achieve the alchemy he had mixed together on his four best films. The screenplays of his last seven pictures were often wanting, and he lost confidence in them. "I wouldn't say that Sam was a connoisseur of fine writing," John Huston said, dissenting from the usual view of Spiegel. "But Sam had good critical faculties, and his greatest talent, I think, was in estimating people, the abilities of others, the degree of their talent. He knew who was a good writer rather than how good his writing was. He knew good direction when he saw it. He had a nose for this sort of thing. He was an extraordinarily fine producer, he could put the factors together and make it work."

He could put the factors together, but he could not make it work on *The Chase*. Although the playwright Lillian Hellman was politically on the blacklist, Spiegel hired her to draft the screenplay from the novel by Horton Foote. The story of a Texan sheriff forced into a strange sympathy with an escaped criminal was a study in continual violence, a savage commentary on the society that had allowed the murder of President John Kennedy in

Dallas. But Spiegel was not satisfied with the Hellman script, which she would not rewrite to his dictates. So he called in another blacklisted writer, Michael Wilson, who again did not provide what Spiegel wanted. The novelist Horton Foote was now summoned and then the script doctor Ivan Moffatt to give the work a final polish. Lillian Hellman was furious at the process. "Decision by democratic majority vote is a fine form of government," she said, "but it's a stinking way to create." Her modest script grew "hot and large, and all the younger ladies in it had three breasts."

The casting of the film brought together a plethora of stars—Marlon Brando, Jane Fonda, Robert Redford, Angie Dickinson and James Fox. Spiegel thought that the casting of Brando would ensure the success of the film: it would be another *On the Waterfront*. Jane Fonda was terrified of acting with Brando, but she admired him for settling for nothing less than the truth of his role. If he sensed something was wrong, he would not agree to do it. So Spiegel had to bring his star together with his final scriptwriter, Ivan Moffatt, in his suite at the Beverly-Wilshire Hotel for a story conference, although he still retired to take "a rest" with his daily girl. Moffatt did not find Brando difficult, but he thought Spiegel tremendously retentive and crablike, a man who would never let anyone go, because he might need him or might be alone. He could not even part with a duplicate script from his desk for fear something was being taken from him, in case someone was escaping his control.

During the shooting of *The Chase* in forty days on a Hollywood back lot simulating a town in Texas, Spiegel did intervene occasionally on the set. He saw in the rushes that Brando's acting had become mannered, his style almost a caricature of realism. Brando was no longer tortured: he had achieved fame. "When he ceased being tortured," Spiegel commented, "he had to pseudotorture himself to function." His inner torment now seemed to be assumed, and neither the abrasive Spiegel nor the mild-mannered director Arthur Penn could provoke their star into agonies and explosions.

Arthur Penn had accepted to direct *The Chase* in a crisis period of his life. His previous film, *Mickey One*, had failed, and he had lost confidence. He felt he had to be orthodox now and make films with studios and producers and film stars and professional screenwriters. He did not fight for the version of the film that he wanted. He allowed the Lillian Hellman script to be rewritten by many hands under Spiegel's supervision. On the set, he told Rex Reed he was "used merely to move the actors through each shot like horses." He also permitted Spiegel to re-edit his fine cut in Europe. This made an artistic disaster of *The Chase*, and Penn took some of the blame. "I left areas open and into those areas other people went and took possession of sections of the film. This wouldn't have happened had I not abdicated." Yet his next venture, *Bonnie and Clyde*, was to prove a magnificent success.

The failure of *The Chase* sent the wrong message to Spiegel. He was persuaded that he had not intervened sufficiently. He was determined totally to control his next film, *The Night of the Generals*, which dealt with the psychopathic Nazi personality that had made him flee Germany thirty years before. His primary concern was with the legal details of what proved to be the first major Anglo-French coproduction ever made. The fine print of such coproductions was complicated, but there were major tax advantages to be had. Long gone were the days when Spiegel was setting up the various offshore Horizon picture companies and sailed so close to the winds of the law that his lawyer Hans Marcus refused to sign legal documents and left him with the statement, "Sam, you can always get out of the country, but I would go to jail." Spiegel often changed his legal representatives, dispensing with one lawyer with the words, "After this, I wouldn't trust you to go and get the duplicate of my birth certificate." He was now represented in the United Kingdom by Irwin Margolies, but Margolies was leaving his law firm to join Warner Brothers. When Spiegel asked a junior partner, Keith Turner, to take over the legal work on the production, Turner refused, saying that there was an unnecessary bending of the rules. To his surprise, Spiegel replied that he had no idea the rules were being bent. "He wanted it regular." Turner was one of the few employees of Spiegel who was trusted and respected, and he continued to work for Horizon Pictures through the next three productions and an aborted one, when the playwright John Osborne was meant to write a script on Charles Dilke, based on the Roy Jenkins biography, with Rex Harrison playing the Victorian politician.

While the legal details of *The Night of the Generals* were being perfected, Spiegel intervened constantly in the scripting and production of the film. He had reached the stage in his life where he would have directed the picture himself if he had the courage, but he did not want to stumble and fall. The screenplay dealt with perverted Nazi generals in Warsaw and Paris, and Spiegel's persistence in changing the script incensed the final screenwriter, Paul Dehn, into commenting, "It was like working with a

Jewish Jesuit." The director, Anatole Litvak, was an old friend of Spiegel's, but could hardly tolerate his producer telling him where to set the camera. Although Peter O'Toole and Omar Sharif both acted well while discharging their *Lawrence* contracts with Spiegel, the final film was disappointing. O'Toole thought that he haunted the film, strutting around in his German uniform and feeling like a tank. But he crushed the other performers in his tracks, just as Spiegel used a steam roller on the creative talents of his screenwriters and director. "All the films he did when he had control," Gottfried Reinhardt commented, "were bad. All he did which were well-packaged were good."

Spiegel himself had lost the courage of his own decisions. The reworked screenplay was not shot by Litvak. He changed it or Spiegel changed it for every new day's shooting. O'Toole blamed Spiegel's interference for the inadequacy of the finished film. He felt that if the original material had been used, it would have been a great film about twisted obsession, a reverse image of the misguided British soldiers building the bridge on the River Kwai. But Spiegel did not have conviction in his own material, only the arrogance to chop and change daily to prove his power and dominance. The producer called the shots; O'Toole recognized that. The moment changes started coming in and people took them seriously, the film began to fall apart. And all of Spiegel's editing and all of Spiegel's orchestration could never put the film together again. Intervention had become his mania and his downfall. His generalship brought on the night.

CHAPTER TWELVE

Another Spiegel

You are partly 100% right.

SAMUEL GOLDWYN

Spiegel had acquired the tricks, the traits, the gait and the vocabulary of dominance. He used his partial deafness to show his dislike of people or bad business, repeating the phrase, "I can't hear you," until the speaker was reduced to repetitive shouting. Equally, he used forgetfulness to deny that something had gone wrong. "I have never heard of the matter," he would declare, "until this moment." He was full of the righteousness of a carefully selective memory. He used his apparent defects as instruments of power.

Yet Spiegel impressed the most intelligent of those who worked with him. Ivan Moffatt has best expressed Spiegel's abiding presence. He had a slow royal strut and the look of a Jewish bullfighter. To those people he liked he gave out warmth like a Sun King. He loved gratuitous giving, particularly to the rich, who did not need his help or his gifts. He behaved like a Roman emperor, especially when mounted on the electrical airport buggies, which he used like chariots without horses. He allied a strange magnetic charm with a glance of understanding, so that most people felt a complicity with him even when he was disagreeing with them. When he talked, he would pause often. His speech came out in sudden gollops. He eked out his phrases, he would not give them away. He always considered what he was saying. "But he did not admit to giving his word."

At the end of the 1960s, the major studios did not admit to their past professions. They refused to back films with large budgets. Even Columbia Pictures looked now to smaller films that appealed to the youth market. *Easy Rider*, the motorcycle and hippie movie starring Peter Fonda and Jack Nicholson, was the wheel of fortune for the future. After failing to make a success of his two previous large-scale movies, Spiegel decided to go with the times, even if they were not to his taste or style. Since *Melba*, he had created only one picture that he had not liked, *Suddenly Last*

Summer, of which he often said, "I wish I didn't make it." But now he agreed to produce or coproduce a number of small pictures for Columbia with a "spectacular" every four years. From 1952 for a decade, he had been convinced that he would "always be able to sense the pulse of the public." Now he would prove that he had lost his touch.

An American producer based in London, Judd Kinberg, had a property that Spiegel allowed to be made under his aegis. *The Happening* was the story of a reformed Mafioso, played by Anthony Quinn, who is kidnapped in Miami by a radical gang of beach boys and girls; he turns the tables on them by proving that he can exploit demands for his ransom better than his captors could. The director, Elliot Silverstein, had made a modish and comic success of a western film, *Cat Ballou*, and he was given total freedom in shooting "this story about the illusion of success." He saw it as a serious drama told in terms of musical comedy. It might be a little bizarre, but it was hard to play safe in the film business. His problem lay in the script, which Spiegel neither supervised nor understood. Wacky comedies were not his bag, nor old Italian ladies saying to their grown sons in trouble, "This too shall pass, if you put your mouth in a smile and get it in gear."

The Happening did provide Faye Dunaway with her debut on screen, but had nothing else to recommend it. The youth market at which it was aimed stayed away in droves. Spiegel decided to wash his hands of contemporary comedy and go for a more serious subject to present through Horizon Pictures for Columbia. He had meant to make a love story from Max Frisch's *Homo Faber* with the same group that made *The Happening*, but its failure led him elsewhere. He chose the John Cheever short story *The Swimmer*, an analysis of the deracination of a man trying to make his way home from one suburban pool to another. To Cheever, a pool was a kind of civilization and pool manners were very involved. His swimmer, Neddy Merrill, was committed to his adventurous and ridiculous pilgrimage, but he could never solve the problems of his life. Eleanor Perry, whose husband Frank Perry directed her screenplays, made four attempts at drafting a script that finally proved acceptable to Spiegel and to the star Burt Lancaster, who declared himself scared to death of the part of the swimmer. "One wrong note," he said, "and it will seem phony." The film was not his usual action picture, which was like a comfortable old suit with a bag of tricks in the pocket.

The Perry team had had one low-budget success, *David and Lisa*, although they had failed with two other independent films after that.

Initially, they were flattered and pleased with Spiegel's lack of intervention and his commitment to a difficult subject. It renewed Frank Perry's faith in the film medium as an art form. But the way the film turned out killed his faith. Spiegel did not like the rushes or the rough cut, nor did Columbia Pictures. After being admirable by his absence from the process of movie-making, Spiegel intervened with a vengeance. Frank Perry had given up his right to a final cut, so legally he "had no bitch". Spiegel said there were too many swimming pools and ordered Perry to shorten the film. In his opinion, there were only fifty-four usable minutes in the rough cut, which should have run for ninety minutes. Three other directors were summoned to work on the picture. The climactic scene in which Barbara Loden tells Burt Lancaster that she has never really enjoyed sex with him was reshot by Sydney Pollack with another actress, Janice Rule. When the film was finally shown, Frank Perry recognised less than fifty percent of his work and thought of running an advertisement in the *New York Times*, saying that *The Swimmer* was not his picture. But he did not like to wash his dirty linen in public. He licked his wounds and resolved never to work for Spiegel again. Hollywood and Hollywood producers were what they were, and when they were involved, "everyone was looking for the brass ring." Only the brass ring was not a good film, it was currying favor with the big man, Spiegel.

The Swimmer turned out to be a relative failure, patchy and inconclusive, lacking both the Perry style and the Spiegel stamp of authority. Spiegel had taken over the project too late. His mind had been elsewhere. He had met a young woman of twenty-two, Ann Pennington, at a viewing of *The Happening* in London. She was working for Judd Kinberg, trying to make a career in the film industry. Well-educated, highly intelligent and attractive, she was escaping from an unhappy marriage. She was sent with legal documents to see Spiegel in Italy in May 1967. They fell in love with one another and cruised on the *Malahne* together throughout that summer, joined by Louis Rheims and his wife, the Van Zuylens, and Freddie Fields with Polly Bergen. The voyage took place at a period in European society when there was a sudden breakthrough of possibilities, where barriers crumbled in social and sexual liberation. Aboard the *Malahne*, the old and the famous met the young and the free in the melting-pot of the 1960s, the era of the Beatles and student revolt. Anything seemed possible.

Ann Pennington became pregnant, and Spiegel insisted that she had the baby. He was intensely jealous of her as he was of anyone who wanted to escape his grasp. In her opinion, jealousy drove him in life. "It was the beginning and the end of his personality." She went to Switzerland during the last months of her pregnancy. He promised to be with her at the birth of his only son, Adam, on the second of June, 1968, but he did not arrive. She ended her relationship with him. "There was always a battle," she said, "because you never knew what to believe. He never did what he said, he had lost the currency of language, so everything had to be in writing. He harrassed me and he became obsessed with Adam. Adam was his Achilles heel."

The lawyer Keith Turner was brought in to make a settlement between them. Ann Pennington had to get a divorce by special permission, while Spiegel remained married to his third wife, Betty, whom he still wanted to control even though they had been separated for thirteen years. Ann forced his hand, and a house was bought for Adam and his mother in Gloucester Crescent in London as part of a settlement. Although Adam's mother insisted on going her own way and escaping Spiegel's tyranny, he tried to break the settlement every time she did not want to do what he wished. As he told his lawyer, "Let her get on with living my life." Her political and social allegiances were always of the left, and he hated her style of living and her friends, although he had to accept her independence. Once he even tried to have Adam taken from her and made a Ward of Court, but he was persuaded that, after all, she was a good mother, while his way of life was hardly suitable for bringing up a small boy. Even so, the fact of having a son changed Spiegel. Adam gave him a new lease on existence. Irene Selznick was on the *Malahne* with Julie Christie and Warren Beatty when the two-year-old was first brought aboard by his nanny. Spiegel sat the child on his lap and fed him with a spoon. None of the guests could believe their eyes. Adam grew into Spiegel's son as they watched. Put down on the deck, the little boy strode forward on strong small legs, his big head protruding, his chest and tummy puffed out, the spitting image of his father. When Billy Wilder went on the yacht and met the child at the age of three, he asked "How do you like the ship, Adam? You like it. It's going to be yours one day." Spiegel was horrified. "Billy, please," he protested "How do we know?"

The coming of Adam made Spiegel refurbish and expand his way of life. He had met Tessa Kennedy as the young wife of Dominic Elwes, with whom she had eloped as an adolescent; now she was married to the producer Elliot Kastner and was a professional interior decorator. He asked her to redo his beloved *Malahne*, as he had no taste for decoration and employed those who did. She received all of four hundred francs for selling off the yacht's old brown furnishings at Spiegel's insistence, then she redecorated the yacht in primary colors, especially bright yellows, with a wall of posters: Spiegel did not travel like the Burtons with his major Impressionist pictures in the stateroom of a boat that might sink. When Spiegel first saw what Tessa Kastner had done to his yacht, he exploded and reduced her to tears, yelling, "The boat is terrible. I don't know it any more." Then his guests praised the new look, and he calmed down and apologized. It was the only time that Tessa Kastner saw Spiegel's courtly manners with women slip. "He embellished everything," she said, with his impeccable taste for suits, wine, food and cigars, "but he screamed at fools."

Spiegel then asked Tessa Kastner to decorate his new villa in Saint-Tropez. She lived on the *Malahne* while working over the house, which was designed to receive the overflow of guests from the yacht and to accommodate Adam and his mother. Spiegel was interested in every detail, but his temper was uncertain. His chauffeur lived in holy terror of him, particularly when Spiegel insisted on driving, an art that he performed on the level of Toad of Toad Hall or Mister Magoo. "Anyone who worked for him," Tessa Kastner said, "was absolutely shaking." Yet he was the genial overseer of his guests, who basked in his hospitality, as long as they allowed him to control their wants and their movements on land and on sea. He was particularly the lord of the telephone. When it rang, the message had to be for him. Even when Jack Nicholson was staying there with the producer Michael White, they would quiver at the sound of the telephone and say to each other, "I hope to God it's not ringing for us."

Many people had cause to remember Spiegel's yacht and villa in the South of France. During his affair with Capucine, William Holden sailed across the Mediterranean and the Atlantic in the *Malahne*; while the romance was fading, Holden took to the bottle again and flung the Oscar he had won into the depths of the ocean. By the time the couple reached the Spiegel Christmas party in Barbados, they were parting and Capucine flew off to Hollywood. In Barbados, Claudette Colbert accepted an invitation to cruise on the *Malahne* back in the Mediterranean and rediscovered yachting blazers and caps she had not worn for thirty years. Yet when she arrived to go aboard she found herself staying at the villa in Saint-Tropez. The only time she ever went aboard the yacht was to have dinner at its moorings in the port. It was too expensive to steam out, and Spiegel never liked a rough sea.

Spiegel's attraction for the rich and the powerful was simple. He did not want anything from them except the privilege of their company. They were not different from him, because he also was rich and powerful. When his guests, indeed, were relatively poor and had been powerful, such as the ex–prime minister Edward Heath, Spiegel gave more than he got. Heath himself was a yachtsman and was famous for compressing his lips to bite back the right command as Spiegel shouted misdirections at his captain when the *Malahne* came in to dock. Heath was also known for keeping his eyes fixed on his copy of Burke or Bagehot when Spiegel's girls were crossing the deck. He refused to see the emperor sometimes had no clothes. As a gourmet and a connoisseur of politics, he relished Spiegel's hospitality and conversation—and also his loyalty to an old friend who had lost his political eminence.

Spiegel's favorite sport was night-long gin rummy. Yet he was known to play tennis. "He was the funniest-looking thing on a tennis court," Evelyn Keyes recalled, "little thin legs, huge belly, nothing at the back. The racket would hang loose by his side till the last moment, then he'd bring it up quickly and whack the ball back." His usual Hollywood doubles partner, Philip Dunne, used to have to run over to return many of the volleys directed at Spiegel's side of the court, only to hear a complaint every time he missed, "What is the matter with you?"

Spiegel was more a voyeur of sports and other people's lives than a participant. In spite of his seagoing yacht and pool at Saint-Tropez, he hardly ever swam. "He could float," Lady Keith noticed, "but very little progress was made." On his annual winter visits to Klosters to stay with Baroness Bentinck and see the Irwin Shaws and Peter Viertel and his wife Deborah Kerr, Spiegel would not ski, although there was precious little else to do in the snow. He brought out Adam, however, and was very proud of his son's first efforts at winter sports. Adam had given him a new reason to live and work forever.

CHAPTER THIRTEEN

The Last Czar

Do you expect a leopard to change his stripes?
SPIEGEL

Spiegel did not want to make a will. He did not want to think of it any more than he wanted to think that he must die. Even though he was in his seventies, he believed in the Californian dream of eternal youth. He could not bear the sight of the illness of others, even though he was sympathetic to them and sent them presents in the hospital. He met Robert Bolt in an elevator soon after Bolt had suffered from a stroke and could not move or speak. Spiegel went white and dumb, and he fled as soon as the elevator door opened. Bolt wanted to comfort Spiegel, to touch him, to tell him not to be so afraid of mortality. There was nothing Spiegel could have done for him except speak to him normally as a friend, but Spiegel had to run away from the sight of the stricken.

As he lived in his magnificence, Spiegel failed to adapt to a changing world. He seemed like the subjects of his two major films of the decade, the last czar of Russia and the last tycoon of Scott Fitzgerald's Hollywood novel. Spiegel said that if he had lived in another era he would have built cathedrals. That was what had attracted him to make the film of *The Bridge on the River Kwai*. In the greatest adversity, a man would build something of such value to him that he would defend it even against his country's interests. "All men want to build cathedrals," Spiegel pronounced. Some did not have the ability, but it did not demand genius. While he spoke to an interviewer, Bridget Byrne, Spiegel seemed to have the look of an innovative pope or aesthetic conquering emperor. "One expects him to be clothed in ermine and armor, not a business suit. The lines of hound dog sadness beneath the eyes balance out the hauteur of the eagle's nose."

Spiegel chose to build his new cathedral on the rubble of the fall of the last czar and czarina. He took three months to decide to buy a biography of *Nicholas and Alexandra*. There was a certain satisfaction in his choice of subject. The Jews of the Russian Pale and the parts of Poland occupied by Russian forces had suffered badly from pogroms under the ultimate czar. Spiegel himself as a boy had seen tens of thousands of refugees flooding through Galicia, and had heard of the czar declaring that the persecution of the Jews was their own fault. It was an ironical retribution to make a film showing the execution of the Russian royal family in much the same way that so many Jewish families had perished during the pogroms of the early years of the century. The czar's chief executioner was a Jew, and many of his assistants were persecuted Letts.

Spiegel turned over the biography of *Nicholas and Alexandra* to the leading Hollywood screenwriter William Goldman. Two years passed as Goldman wrote and rewrote the script to Spiegel's requirements. "I believe pictures are rewritten, not written," he said. "Goldman was desperate many times. I had to convert him to believe that each rewrite improved the original. Now he is blissfully happy." Neither the repeated work nor the reputed happiness showed in the final version of the script, which was laborious dramatized history, with a Rasputin more devil than mad monk. Spiegel once again lost confidence in the final draft five weeks before shooting was due to begin in Spain. He sent for Eddie Chodorov, who was then living in Paris, and offered him fifty thousand dollars to fix the script. "Not classy enough," Spiegel said. "There's something wrong with it." Chodorov needed the money, but refused the assignment. He asked for five months to change the historical stereotypes into human beings. The English playwright Edward Bond accepted the job of polishing the dialogue of the Russian Revolution and is credited with creating the immortal line, "Stalin, I'm Lenin, I want you to meet Trotsky."

Spiegel took his usual care and time over casting. He was overwhelmed by the ingratitude and high prices demanded by the stars whom he felt he had made, saying of Peter O'Toole that he had ceased to be an actor when he thought he was a star. Spiegel took pleasure and profit in casting two unknowns in the leading roles, Michael Jayston and Janet Suzman. "It is a joy to create them," he said, "and, in doing so, to deflate those who feel that they dominate the domain. My pleasure is, of course, shortlived. It is inevitable that they, too, become unbearable."

Not only the casting of actors, but also of directors, technicians and a composer took up Spiegel's time and attention. There was a succession of directors before the choice of Franklin Schaffner, a professional without the touch of magic. Spiegel told his casting director, Maud Spector, to bring him the best of British talent, and he cast from them, giving his time and respect, only seeing two in an afternoon rather than forty in the assembly line of a modern film audition. "Very inspiring," Maud Spector recalled. "Bloody murder. Kept everyone waiting for hours. But all was made up by his dreadful charm." She was herself a professional and knew the adage that in the film industry, you are paid to be inconvenienced.

The casting of the czar's young daughters was particularly Spiegel's concern. "I'd send in the young girls," Maud Spector said. "I'd say, Sam likes young girls. You say you have a boy friend. Not all of them did. Some were even disappointed that Sam didn't chase them round the room." Spiegel was particularly interested in casting the adolescent Lynne Frederick, who later became the wife of Peter Sellers. She played the czar's daughter who best survived the filming of the Russian Revolution.

Nicholas and Alexandra was shot mainly in Madrid, where General Franco was still in charge. It was a far cry from the Bolshevik upheaval that had helped to make Spiegel run over so many frontiers into so many countries. He had an explanation, as usual, for his choice of subject and location. The Russian Revolution had been the moment "when we said farewell to the world that was—with free and easy access to all parts of it. From that moment on the world was divided into two." That was why the film was being shot in Spain by the American Schaffner, another director to have such stupendous quarrels with Spiegel that Leo Jaffe of Columbia Pictures had to be called to arbitrate between them. Spiegel was trying to recreate the conflict and the tension that had brought out the best in the films he had created with David Lean. "No good film can be made," he used to say, "without screaming and abrasiveness."

Lord Louis Mountbatten, a relative of the last czar and czarina, was emotionally shattered when he saw *Nicholas and Alexandra* at the premiere in London. He had been pledged to the czar's second daughter, Tatiana, and the uncanny resemblance of the young actress who played her made him weep. At the party afterward, with a Russian orchestra playing, he told the actress, "You should have been my wife," then danced madly till dawn to drive off the depression of the royal massacre. But the images that had moved him failed to move the critics, who universally disliked the film, calling it boring and heavy. Even Spiegel recognized his failure and fell into the gloom that Mountbatten had tried to dissipate.

Spiegel blamed Chodorov for the lack of success of *Nicholas and Alexandra*. His friend had refused to put the script right. "I can't forgive you," he told Chodorov in the London office of Horizon Pictures. "You were disloyal to me. I needed you and you turned your back on me." Chodorov was frightened that Spiegel would turn his back on him forever, so he looked down on Spiegel's desk and saw a copy of the biography lying there. "Did you let William Goldman write his version of the script from the biography?" he asked. "Or did you tell him to write it the way you wanted it?" Now Spiegel did turn his back on Chodorov to think of an answer. "Do you expect a leopard to change his stripes?" he asked. Chodorov laughed. "Spots, Sam, spots. A leopard has spots." Spiegel swung his chair around to declare himself. "Truthfully, I would rather make a bad picture and make it my way, than make a good picture and make it your way."

His expensive failure ended Spiegel's long relationship with Columbia. It had lasted since the making of *On the Waterfront*. Spiegel used to boast that Columbia Pictures in London was a mere offshoot of his Horizon Pictures, and that now his agreement had ended, he would at last be able to make the pictures he really wanted to make. Of course, he had mostly made the pictures he really wanted to make. Even if he was in his seventies, he felt that there might be new beginnings or returns. Although he was still gloomy about shooting pictures in Hollywood, where he said that most of those making movies would be better occupied crating oranges, he was tempted by Scott Fitzgerald's novel *The Last Tycoon*, centering on a character who was based on Irving Thalberg but who had characteristics of Spiegel himself. It was certainly the only classic American work of fiction that took a Hollywood producer as its hero.

Spiegel's choice of a screenwriter was both brilliant and bizarre. He chose Harold Pinter, England's premier playwright, who did not know Hollywood well. Spiegel had long admired Pinter's craft. They had nearly cooperated with Joseph Losey on *Accident*, but Spiegel had withdrawn, not liking the final screenplay. "You call this a script?" he said to Pinter. "But it doesn't begin. Nothing happens. People won't understand it. The cinema is a popular medium. You just come into an accident. Who are their fathers? Their mothers? You don't tell people anything." When the film *Accident* was a success, Spiegel did not change his mind about the screenplay. He wanted Pinter to write *The Last Tycoon* for him, because Pinter knew nothing of Spiegel's background in the film industry in the 1930s. "I really tried to extricate myself from my own recollections and reminiscences," Spiegel said. He chose Pinter because the writer had few preconceptions about Hollywood. Consequently, he could assess the attitudes of Scott Fitzgerald rather than bringing in any nostalgia of his own as Spiegel would have done. *The Last Tycoon* was "about movies at their grandest, if not their best. And it's set in a time when they were part of America's bloodstream." Spiegel insisted that he did not see himself as Monroe Stahr, the last tycoon of the novel, but he did want to say something about the changes in Hollywood since he began in the business. In the mid-1970s the studios were all lawyers and accountants listening to the cash register and producing quantity, quantity, quantity for television. Once there had been a period "when picture making was really a matter of life and death for Hollywood people". It certainly had been for S. P. Eagle.

Mike Nichols was chosen to direct the film. It was the first of two attempts by Spiegel, Pinter and Nichols to work together, and both ended with Nichols walking away, finding such a collaboration impossible. While writing *The Last Tycoon*, Pinter took refuge in Spiegel's apartment in Grosvenor Square. He was in the process of divorcing the actress Vivien Merchant before his marriage to the writer Antonia Fraser, the wife of Sir Hugh Fraser. He admired Spiegel for caring about all the four people who were involved. "He made no moral judgement whatsoever," Pinter said. "He knew everyone suffered in such circumstances."

Pinter worked with relish on the screenplay with Mike Nichols and Spiegel wherever the producer happened to be, in Los Angeles, New York or London. Spiegel even added one of Nichols's sons to his list of eighty-eight godchildren to bind the director more closely to him. But Nichols could not stand the pressure, the interference, the endless demands for revisions of the script. Pinter was called over to New York to prevent a walkout by Nichols. "I can't live with this black shadow over my shoulder," Nichols complained. "I feel like a little boy, I'm going to go mad." Spiegel could not persuade Nichols to continue, but still wanted to pick his brains about the screenplay. Pinter now raged, saying he did not want the shreds of such wisdom, and threatened to leave the project as well. Spiegel put his hand to his chest. "You want to kill me, you want to break my heart?"

Pinter stayed to go on working on the script of *The Last Tycoon* for more than a year. He had infinite patience, Spiegel said, and brought freshness to the project, waking up Spiegel's ideas. That was literally so. He and Nichols had an inspiration for the ending of the picture, that Monroe Stahr should again demonstrate how to tell a story in a movie. Their inspiration occurred when Spiegel had retired for a massage: Pinter's enthusiasm led him to interrupt Spiegel's bedroom therapy; but when the ruffled Spiegel appeared in his silk dressing-gown and heard Pinter's ending, he sank down serenely into an armchair, again clutched his heart and said, "You have made me so happy." All else paled into insignificance. An aesthetic thrill—Pinter said—had overcome any other thrill Spiegel might have been feeling.

True to his style, Pinter's screenplay was full of silences and inter-ruptions. He remained faithful to Fitzgerald's novel, hardly adding to the unfinished work. He needed to flesh out the dream woman Kathleen and to dramatise the conflict between Stahr and the old studio boss Brady—a struggle based on Thalberg's quarrels with Eddie Mannix and Louis B. Mayer. As Pauline Kael wrote when she criticized the finished film, Pinter did not supply what was missing. His art was the art of taking away. "And less can be less."

With Mike Nichols leaving the film Spiegel went back to Kazan to direct for him. The reason that Spiegel had not approached him in the first place was that Kazan had dedicated himself to writing novels and his previous three pictures had been failures. Yet Spiegel did not know another director who was as skillful as Kazan at releasing an actor from his inhibitions. Kazan did not need this skill in working with Robert de Niro, who played Monroe Stahr to the strength and suaveness born, nor did he need to instruct Ray Milland, who had acted for Thalberg, nor Robert Mitchum as Brady, nor Jack Nicholson and Tony Curtis and Jeanne Moreau, but he had his work cut out trying to get a performance from the unknown actress that Spiegel insisted on casting in the role of Kathleen Moore— the British producer's daughter, Ingrid Boulting. She could not suggest the depths and resonances and threats and menaces that lay behind Pinter's sparse words and pauses. In de Niro's opinion, Kazan was more Medi-terranean in feeling than Pinter. He created an interesting tension by always trying to play against Pinter's restraint, but he did not dare to add to Pinter's words. He could only create tension with experienced and hungry actors—Tony Curtis particularly, playing the important role of a great screen lover, gave a performance of such vitality that it was better than anything he had done since *The Sweet Smell of Success*. Ingrid Boulting, however, could not suggest anything more than a sweet and pretty presence. Her meaningful pauses were like a light going out.

Both Spiegel and Kazan agreed on the film that they were trying to make. Spiegel called it a gentle picture. In the seventies, people were trying to outdo each other in shock and horror films, as if shock therapy would cure the ills of the movie business. But the danger of electroshock therapy was that the treatment had to be stronger every time. "You've got to keep scaring them more, and where's the limit?" *The Last Tycoon* was what Kazan declared it to be—deliberately *adagio* and elegiac, full of throwaway detail like the ketchup bottle among the silverware in the studio executive dining-room. Ray Milland, playing the wolfish studio lawyer, remembered Hollywood in the 1930s as a colorful and exciting place, where stars looked and dressed like stars. And even Kazan admitted that the top producers of the time were larger than life, as Spiegel was himself, "vain old charismatic Hollywood monsters," obsessed with making the best picture of that year because it had their name on it.

The Last Tycoon was far from being the best picture of 1975, and it did have Spiegel's name on it. While the critics on the East Coast praised Pinter's faithful script, Kazan's direction and Robert de Niro's magisterial performance, the critics on the West Coast called the movie both laconic and swollen, all pauses and hot air. The mixed criticism and commercial flop of the film drove Spiegel into a kind of despair. His old friend, the distributor Max Youngstein, found him very damaged more than hurt. He tried to be philosophical about it, saying of the casting of Ingrid Boulting, "Sometimes you make a mistake, sometimes you succeed." He thought the film an honest failure, but recognized that perhaps he had lost touch with what was working in the industry at the time. Old Hollywood was not new Hollywood, and he could not reign there in studios run by corporation lawyers and committee decisions. He was truly the last film czar, if not the last tycoon.

CHAPTER FOURTEEN

The Betrayal of Mortality

*Death is an unwelcome interference
with the life plan*
SPIEGEL

Spiegel did not believe in mortality as far as he was concerned; he had survived so much. He did know betrayal—the countries and hopes and people who had betrayed him, and whom he had betrayed in return. The Jews in Poland had been betrayed by the Austrians and the Russians and the Poles. The First World War had betrayed Spiegel by its persecution and its impoverishment. Pioneer Palestine had deceived him with its hardship and its threadbare dreams. America and Germany, Austria and England, France and Mexico had condemned him and deported him. His very mother had loved his older brother more than her younger son. He had betrayed his first wife and baby daughter, to make money and to do well. He had falsified finance and shortchanged friends in his quest for success in the cinema. The fortune that flowed from his best films allowed him to show his generosity and good taste to hundreds of friends and hundreds of millions of moviegoers. Now, finally, the people no longer wanted to see the good movies that he still was making, while his aging flesh was betraying his longing for eternal youth and immortality.

"There has been a dreadful tragedy," declared Spiegel one evening aboard the *Malahne* to his dinner guests including the American ambassador to London, David Bruce, his wife Evangeline and Diana Phipps, who had first seen Spiegel while staying at Count Bismarck's on Capri. Having been called away to the communications room, Spiegel returned to the table looking very mournful. "It will have worldwide repercussions—it's catastrophic." From his doomladen tone, the guests naturally assumed that a third world war must be imminent. David Bruce rose, expecting an immediate recall to London. "Sharon Tate has been murdered," said Spiegel. "That's Hollywood now for you." At this unexpected revelation, there were sighs of relief and the odd nervous smile from the guests, none of whom knew who Sharon Tate was. It seemed to some that Spiegel had lost his sense of proportion—Armageddon was not nigh, as they had supposed—for few could have known that the horrible murder of the young actress who was Roman Polanski's wife reminded Spiegel of his own mortality.

Diana Phipps was also at a dinner on the *Malahne* with the writers Joan Didion and John Gregory Dunne, when Spiegel declared, "I believe I have led the most dissolute life of the four of us." None of the others disagreed. Spiegel's dissoluteness was an incessant denial of his age as well as a gratification of his senses. Taken to a nude encounter club in New York by a woman friend of the Earl of Dudley, she was surprised to see the bare, portly old Spiegel lost under a heap of naked girls after a quarter of an hour. At a party given by Romy Schneider's husband, Baroness Stephanie von Watzdorf was equally surprised to see Spiegel sitting with a tall blonde on his knee, who turned out to be a female impersonator with a bass voice. Spiegel could not keep out of the trends of the times. He had to experience everything. When a group of young actresses was taking acid and mescaline on board the *Malahne* at the end of the 1970s, Spiegel said with regret, "I never had that. I missed the sixties." He was given a tab or two to take and loved the result, first looking at the stars and then driving the girls very slowly to the local nightclub in Saint-Tropez with the tedious caution of the stoned. As he entered the club with the girls, all the people parted in front of him like the Red Sea. To Corinthia West, who saw him there, Spiegel seemed "so happy, like a child among the lilies of the field."

In spite of his pleasures, Spiegel was becoming more tyrannical, remote, demanding and lonely. He made his friends work for his hospitality. Some of them found him intriguing as a powerful bully, a frightening Roman emperor, who could be easily bored and switch off his attention if not entertained. One said: "You were expected to keep in touch daily with him wherever he was in the world. He wanted always to know what you were doing. He had the gift of making you feel obliged to him when he had neglected you." He could be arrogant and dismiss people, he could be sympathetic and a good listener, he could not be ignored. People always clustered around him. He had a dry sense of humor, full of oblique references to the human condition, and he appeared to care about the theater, the cinema, the ballet, music, literature, art and politics, about which he had a world view. He knew the great experts and the famous names, he used their judgments and made them his own. His powers of recollection were extraordinary, yet he was unlike other old men. He would not reminisce about the past. He preferred talking about the present and the future, as though these were all of life, all to live for. "He would not go down Memory Lane," his friend Michael White recalled. For Spiegel had too much to deny and forget.

He could not, however, forget his growing son Adam. He selected a new lawyer, Mark Littman, to become the child's trustee and arrange for the disposition of his estate. Littman recognized Spiegel's life-force and need to dominate, to emasculate any young man who was near the young girl he wanted to impress. Although he was obsessed with Adam, he was incapable of fulfilling the proper duties of a parent. One day he told his son, "I was not born to be a father." Yet he grew closer and closer to Adam as the boy became a young man very much in his image, if not in his character. "He found it quite difficult to display his emotions," Adam said. "But it was lovely when he did. He was so cold a lot of the time, but when it was warm, it seemed all the warmer." There was a clash between father and son, when Adam revolted from his father's possessive autocracy and refused to go to boarding school. But Spiegel compromised with his son, recognizing his own assertion as a young man, his own rebellion from his family that had sent him to Palestine as a young pioneer. He sent Adam to work on a *kibbutz* in Israel. "He used me to make himself younger," Adam said. "He liked to stride into a party with me or a young girl on his arm. He was a very self-conscious man, very unwilling to talk about his past." Yet through him, Adam met all his father's friends and felt that he knew his father better than any other person at the end.

Spiegel also had to compromise in his attempts to control the life of Adam's mother. She had gone to the Royal Academy of Dramatic Arts because she had always wanted to be an actress, although her parents had insisted that she went to a university. She was always working, both as an actress and an Assistant Director at the Royal Court Theater under Stuart Burge. Eventually, she married the brilliant new artistic director of the Royal Court, Max Stafford-Clark. Unlike Spiegel's third wife Betty, whom he kept endlessly on the hook by even putting her house in his name, Ann Pennington broke free from his dominance and jealousy and made her own life. She only regretted all the battles over Adam, which had consumed her energy and emotions. Increasingly, she found that Adam identified with her and her passion for the world of the theater. In that way, he was gratifying his father's wish: "God forbid he should go into the film business—I hope he chooses something less moribund."

Ann Pennington did not see the generosity that Spiegel showed to friends and strays who sought his help. She thought he behaved well to those who did not know him well to justify his sense of himself. The problem was that he had no permanent sense of values, no code to govern his conduct at all. He preferred acting the whimsical tyrant, living in confusion, giving presents and then demanding them back. He kept people close to him by making them uncertain of his favors. Only when Spiegel died was Ann Pennington liberated from his constant supervision. "I feel so relieved," she said, "I will never hear his voice on the phone again."

Spiegel's own film career did indeed seem on the point of dying. He was summoned to salvage rather than create by an old friend and enemy. After his expensive failure *Ryan's Daughter*, David Lean had been working for six years on a remake of *Mutiny on the Bounty*. With Robert Bolt as his screenwriter, he wanted to tell the story in two parts at a cost of fifty million dollars. The first part would be the actual account of the mutiny; the second part would deal with what happened to the crew on their return to England. Dino de Laurentiis was producing the film for Warner Brothers with American executive assistants. An unholy financial mess had been created; as in the film of *The Producers*, more than one hundred per cent appeared to have been given away in profit participations. A replica of H.M.S. *Bounty* had been built at the cost of two million dollars in New Zealand and lay beached there. Then Robert Bolt had a stroke, the American executives and Warner Brothers pulled out, and de Laurentiis lost interest. Remembering past successes and forgetting past quarrels, Lean went back to Spiegel to salvage the project. Lean seemed to accept that only the first part of the picture would be made as Spiegel could not see people going back to view the second part—nor could he raise the financing to film two linked pictures.

As it was, Spiegel renegotiated all the contracts and budgets to make possible the financing of *Mutiny on the Bounty*. Christopher Reeve, fresh from his success in *Superman*, was chosen to play Mr. Christian. Melvyn Bragg was selected to rewrite the Bolt script as one screenplay, set in Tahiti. As Spiegel described it, the film would "focus on the impact on the lives of a disciplined English crew when they became part of a South Sea existence." Bragg agreed with Spiegel that Mr. Christian was a villain, but Lean saw him as a nautical Lawrence, a virtuous young man. There were terrible quarrels over the script with both Spiegel and Lean clutching their hearts and accusing the other of murder. The dispute ended with

Lean declaring that he would rewrite the script himself. He knew exactly what Spiegel wanted. In a state of euphoria, Spiegel announced in Los Angeles in May 1980 that the shooting of *Mutiny on the Bounty* would begin in a month; he had arranged for a major studio to back it.

Spiegel, however, had forgotten the script. When Lean returned with his final version, it was the original Bolt screenplay in two parts, somewhat revised. Fresh quarrels broke out between the two old men, as had happened on past projects. The final explosion came when Spiegel allowed himself to take twenty telephone calls during a conference with Lean, who stormed out, damned if he would tolerate so many interruptions. Spiegel was diplomatic about the final breach, taking some of the blame himself. He said the subject would be terribly exhausting to film. Lean liked that sort of thing. "He is a man with no particular roots in any country."

One *Lawrence of Arabia* was enough for Spiegel. He tried to make Lean give up *Mutiny on the Bounty* and do something else with him, but the subject was an *idée fixe* with Lean, who spent more years of frustration working on it until he finally yielded and made *Passage to India* instead. Spiegel had himself begun to count the years left to him for creating another major motion picture. He was nearly eighty years old, and *Mutiny on the Bounty* would have taken up four years of his remaining life. "Do I want to spend my last four years in the Pacific Ocean?" he asked Tessa Kastner, and answered for himself that he did not think he did.

Thus Spiegel might never have made another film, if he had not seen Harold Pinter's play *Betrayal* with Mike Nichols in New York. Spiegel did not like the performance of the actors, saying, "When Americans play Englishmen, they are more papal than the pope." But at dinner after the performance, Antonia Fraser asked Spiegel on impulse why he shouldn't make a picture from *Betrayal*. "Who would go and see such a film?" Spiegel asked the playwright himself. And Pinter answered, "It's about adultery. They'll see it all over the world."

Although the script of the film derived very much from the play, its translation to the screen was complex, Spiegel knew that: "A love affair, a *ménage à trois*, told backwards, from the moment of its collapse to its conception." It was not a cynical play about the impermanence of love, but it was the first film since David Lean's *Brief Encounter* to deal with very few characters "locked into an emotional situation that has taken control of their lives". In fact, love relationships did not stay on the same level. When a relationship changed, Spiegel thought that it had to be done with honesty. "If you betray honesty, you ruin things."

For the second time, Mike Nichols gave up working on the script with Pinter and Spiegel, and he flatly refused to direct the film. Against his better judgment, he had been bullied by Spiegel to fly across the American continent to meet Jeremy Irons, who was arriving on the *Queen Elizabeth II* and was cast to play the lead in the film. The trip was superfluous and Nichols was kept from seeing his family by Spiegel's cajolery. He could not tolerate his producer's power in making him do what he did not want to do. Pinter called Spiegel's persistence in getting his own way "a burrowing, bulldoggish thing that never let you go". Yet he respected working with Spiegel closely on the script, however demanding he was because he was right so often. Once Pinter suggested that the opening scene should be played during a walk by the Serpentine rather than in a pub. "What is Serpentine?" Spiegel asked. "Birds? Fish? Why not a pub?" And so it was in the beginning of the film.

After her success playing with Jeremy Irons in Pinter's adaptation of *The French Lieutenant's Woman*, Spiegel wanted Meryl Streep to act the woman's role in the film. Streep said she would play, then changed her mind because her family life depended on her staying in the United States, "and you can't make this picture anywhere else but in England". There was no question of transferring *Betrayal* to an American setting, because Spiegel found the texture of the play and screenplay so English, particularly all the reticence in the face of provocation. "For the emotions not to erupt constantly is only conceivable—not necessarily possible, but conceivable—in England." Certainly Spiegel in London erupted constantly in the face of provocation, although not to Pinter. In their relationship, Pinter said, "I was the erupter."

Spiegel now approached the French director Louis Malle to take over from Mike Nichols. But Malle declined the offer. The subject dismayed him. "*Betrayal* is all about the mortality of love," Spiegel said. But when he talked to Malle, the French director was having an affair with Candice Bergen, who later married him. "When a man is infatuated with a woman," Spiegel observed, "it is not time to talk about how love dies." Eventually, an Artistic Director of the Royal Shakespeare Company, David Jones, was given the assignment. At first, he thought it necessary to appear absolutely impregnable to Spiegel, although he was racked with doubts. But when he learned that his confidence was driving Spiegel crazy, he showed himself "anxious and worried when he was about, and then he was marvellously supportive".

The casting of *Betrayal* was completed with Ben Kingsley, fresh from playing the lead in Spiegel's old project on Gandhi, and the lesser-known Patricia Hodge. Spiegel backed the whole production himself. *The Last Tycoon* had been financed by selling off world distribution rights to three companies, but *Betrayal* took $3,000,000 out of the revenues of Horizon Pictures. It was a personal investment for Spiegel, a small film, not a large one, but even making a small film cost too much in 1982. He resented being told that *Betrayal* was a little subject compared to blowing up bridges or desert wars. "Is it really?" he said. "Do you worry in a painting about the size of the canvas?"

The picture was made well, but its canvas was not large enough to succeed outside New York. Pinter was summoned to Manhattan for press conferences and discovered to his fury that Spiegel had betrayed him, telling the journalists that *Betrayal* was founded on Pinter's own experiences. "Nonsense," Pinter replied, "it's founded on Spiegel's life." However that was, Pinter revered the old man and admired his total dedication in making a film on all levels—something he required of his associates. Pinter had the same dedication as a writer, if not in all the processes of making a film. But Spiegel was the man fully behind the picture to the very end. Sidney Sapir, who handled the world sales of *Betrayal*, was summoned to a four-hour conference with Spiegel in his apartment in Grosvenor House. There he found his first "bright-eyed and bushy-tailed octogenarian". Spiegel's great attention to detail, however, his incisive and ever-active mind, his intelligence and his tenacity amazed Sapir, who would have found these qualities rare in a man of forty.

Even in his eighties, Spiegel's vigor and energy were astounding. He did not believe that he would die. He had a greed for living. "Death," he told his friend Lord Weidenfeld, "is an unwelcome interference with the life plan." Although he sold the *Malahne* because it was too expensive to maintain, he refurbished his penthouse in New York and bought a new apartment in Grosvenor Square. His adviser on decoration, Diana Phipps, found him lonely and inescapable, but possessed with an extraordinary power and craftiness. He had only bought the lease of the new London place because she had found it for him and agreed to redo it. He clutched at the company of beautiful women he could employ and control: it was almost impossible to say goodbye to him on any evening when he might find himself alone. She had to fight him tooth and nail over every change to his Manhattan headquarters, which was all marble and protuberances in its Edward Durrell Stone building. She had to storm at him in the confrontations that were his meat and drink. "Either this table goes or I do," she would shout at him. "It's my own money," he would scream back. The only way to get what she wanted was to make a scene. He loved it and was totally charming once he had reduced her to a wreck. After their biggest battle, he suddenly declared, "I have more of a past than I have of a future." She was his slave after that.

In his eighties Spiegel began to give up his conveyor belt of young women. When Melvyn Bragg visited him at his New York apartment, Spiegel could not even remember the first names of the girls passing through by night and day. "Melvyn, this is Miss ... um ... and this is Miss ... ah ... leaving." But finally after 1983, he lived regularly in New York with a young ballet dancer of nineteen, Jennifer Kent, of intelligence and grace with the fine-boned feline face of the French film stars of the 1930s. He had met her when she was living with five other girls in a walk-up apartment, had set her up in her own place, had made her give up dancing and take up drama lessons and had insisted that he loved her and that she should stay with him. "Don't do anything else," he said to her. "Don't choose anything, unless you want it so much you don't eat to get it." He was continually on the telephone to her drama teachers and her parents, trying to direct her every movement. Whenever she tried to break away from his possessiveness, he would beg her to return to him. Every Thanksgiving Day, he would go with her to dinner at her parents' house in upstate New York. He would not let her go, and his face would light up when he found her waiting for him when he came home from his celebrity parties in New York. Although he was seeing everybody of importance, she knew of his terrible loneliness and could not assuage it with her love.

He took her to Vienna for the Christmas of 1983. He had not been there since he had been a young man and a refugee from Galicia. They stayed at Sacher's Hotel, and he visited the aristocratic Austrian relations of Diana Phipps. He did not claim to them any background in Vienna, but he returned one afternoon to the hotel with his face glowing. He had envisioned his final film. In it, he could manufacture his Viennese past. It would be the story of a family in the city, divided between the Great Powers at the end of the Second World War. He would relive his experiences in Vienna and say what he thought about the Communist occupation of Eastern Europe. The scope of the film would be greater than Graham Greene's *The Third Man*, and he hired the historian Hugh Thomas to write a treatment of the subject in the form of a novel.

Lord Thomas found himself embroiled in the Spiegel habits of procrastination. For the next two years, he had to write draft after draft, eight hundred pages in all, for someone he considered a prince of wasting time. But Spiegel still felt that he had all the time in the world ahead of him. Not until he was eighty-four did his incredible health and vigor begin to deteriorate. He did not forsee his death. He convinced Jennifer Kent as he convinced all his friends that he was an inescapable part of existence. He claimed to her to have a third eye, an intuition for films, for people and the future. He knew what would succeed, what would happen. Above all, he knew where all his friends were and what they were doing. It was impossible to break away from him. If he ever died, he would leave a gap in nature.

He filled the lives of the hundreds who knew him, and yet everyone stayed within a compartment, licensed by Spiegel to meet only others in that group. Celebrity met celebrity, family met family, lovers met only him. Ringmaster extraordinary, Spiegel controlled his small worlds. He was, as Dennis van Thal said, a great impresario of other people's lives. He ran his dinner parties as if they were classes: all conversation was directed to him at the head of the table. If any of the courtesies or formalities were neglected, he could rage as if he were Attila the Hun. Yet he soon forgot his anger and forgave the breach of etiquette almost immediately: for he did not want to lose his friends. He even held one last New Year's Eve party in Hollywood, although he disliked the place because it did not grant him the respect that he felt he deserved. He dressed up as a pageboy with a ruffled shirt for the benefit of all the generations who were there: Robert de Niro and Ryan O'Neal, Warren Beatty and Jack Nicholson, Groucho Marx and Spiegel's old friend, Max Youngstein, who gave him a final valedictory. "You accepted Sam in total, you didn't accept him piece by piece. You knew he was a mixture of good and bad, but he had style, a kind of courage, an innate ability to handle things that other people could not handle without showing their nervousness."

He became increasingly ill and deaf in 1985, finally undergoing a prostate operation in London before Christmas. He could not admit to the diminishing of his powers or his body, although he became extremely dependent on his London physician, Doctor Sachs, who was summoned every second day in case there was pollen in the air and Spiegel caught a cold. He still went to parties continually and gave them. He would not be left alone. Finally, he flew to Saint Martin in the Virgin Islands to see in the New Year with friends, the Peabodys and the Rayners and the Ustinovs. Twenty years previously during the filming of *Lawrence of Arabia*, Robert Bolt had asked Peter O'Toole how he thought Spiegel would die. With Celtic insight, O'Toole had replied: "Spiegel will die in two inches of bathwater." And so it was, on New Year's Eve, the day when Spiegel normally gave a party himself, he died from a sudden heart attack, alone in his hotel room, falling into a bath, obliged to nobody, the way he wished to die, if he had to go. Peter Ustinov was present while a young American doctor tried to revive the dead Spiegel by pummeling his great chest. "Give him the kiss of life," the doctor told Ustinov, who demurred from doing the useless act. "Alive or dead," he said, "I would not kiss Sam Spiegel."

Spiegel's third wife, Betty, flew out to Saint Martin to bring back the body to New York. She was proud of being Mrs. Spiegel and believed that her husband would always be part of her life, however separately they had lived. In the American way of death, the body was laid out at Frank E. Campbell's Funeral Chapel on Madison Avenue and 81st Street. There his friends paid him a last visit. Radie Harris of the *Hollywood Reporter* found the occasion like a celebrity gathering for a premiere: Warren Beatty with Karen Lerner, Arthur and Alexandra Schlesinger, Mica and Ahmet Ertegun, Geraldine Fitzgerald and Stuart Scheftel, Shirley and Robert Lantz, Phyllis Newman and Adolph Green, Betty Comden, Mike Nichols, Irene Mayer Selznick, Budd Schulberg, Leo Jaffe, George Stevens, Irving Lazar, Eunice Kennedy Shriver, Jean Kennedy Smith, Nan Kempner and many others. Spiegel was buried after a service conducted by a rabbi in a nonsectarian chapel. His son Adam Spiegel read the 23rd Psalm, and Arthur Schlesinger gave a moving address, saying that those present must feel that an era had ended. Movies had begun and flourished as an industry—and an art—dominated by mighty personalities:

> Sam Spiegel was the last of the giants. His death marks the end of a great chapter in the history of the cinema.... He brought to the making of movies the passion of a true artist. A film, he used to say, penetrates all frontiers. It reaches more people in a lifetime than a Renaissance painter could in a millennium. Sam had a high sense of responsibility

to the medium and exacting standards for it: and he poured his own blazing vision of quality into a remarkable series of movies. He worked with the most brilliant talents of his day ... and he drove them relentlessly. The constant pressure often exasperated, sometimes enraged. But, when the ordeal was over, his collaborators recognized that Sam's perfectionism had goaded them into bringing out the best in themselves.

In his memorial speech, Schlesinger also recognized that Spiegel remained a mysterious and intensely private man. His life had many strands and friends, and he tended to keep them carefully apart. They all encountered each other for the first and final time as guests at the Park Avenue apartment after the burial service. They were under the aegis of James Higgins, Spiegel's longtime butler and confidant. The family all met together at last—Rachel and the daughter, Alisa, and her daughter; Spiegel's niece, Raya Dreben, the executor of his will and a judge in Massachusetts; Betty Spiegel and Ann Pennington and Adam Spiegel; but not Spiegel's brother, Shalom, nor his mother, Regina, who had both died in Israel, she at the age of ninety-four. Jennifer Kent was there, wandering lonely in the crowd. The staff of Columbia and Horizon Pictures was there, particularly Spiegel's assistant Pat Ricci. Also present was the host of friends and celebrities, many of whom did not know that the others knew the secretive Spiegel. Twenty small groups and individuals moved from room to room in the penthouse, hardly recognizing one another.

There was a dispute about an appropriate memorial service for Spiegel in London. Some of his close friends wanted extracts from his films to be shown at the National Film Theatre with memorial addresses between the clips. But religious advice prevailed, and the service was held in the West London Synagogue with speeches by Lord Weidenfeld, Edward Heath and Harold Pinter, whose tribute to Spiegel was most just.

Spiegel made four major films in his time and a number of other very good ones. I see the four major ones as *On the Waterfront, The African Queen, The Bridge on the River Kwai* and *Lawrence of Arabia*. It is an extraordinary achievement. I worked with him on two screenplays, *The Last Tycoon* and *Betrayal*, and when I say that he *made* all these films, I mean what I say. He clearly didn't write them or direct them but he took responsibility for them, in the most minute detail, from conception to execution—all the way along the line. Total responsibility. Total dedication.

We became very close friends. In the worst crisis of my life it was to Sam that I turned and it was Sam who gave me shelter.

While he was a very "knowing" person, he remained an optimist. He believed that the human spirit would prevail over the destructive forces within it. I think that these lines of Philip Larkin would have meant a great deal to him:

> Reaching for the world, as our lives do,
> As all lives do, reaching that we may give
> The best of what we are and hold as true:
> Always it is by bridges that we live.

We shall remember him for so many things, but I feel, as much as anything else, for the twinkle in his eye.

Pinter knew Spiegel as well as any man at the end. He seemed almost a father. He was a man of strongly-held views, passionate about the human spirit overcoming adversity. "How it flowers. How it blooms. Survival. I think he knew about that." Spiegel also felt very strongly about his Jewishness. He had been part of the survival of the Jews and their spirit in adversity. When his will came to be read, he acquitted his debt to his Jewish origin and to his enduring, if muted, attachment to Israel and Jerusalem by donating a large sum of money derived from the sale of his paintings to the Israel Museum in Jerusalem. So his life came full circle and in his character, as in any Baroque work with its convolutions, complexities, distortions and discordances, there was a final resolution. Worth some $25 million, he did not die especially wealthy, for he had spent generously all his life, giving to his friends his good fortune and his taste.

Spiegel was the last of the old creative producers, the heir of Alexander Korda and Sam Goldwyn, of Irving Thalberg and David Selznick. The cinema was his dedication, and he set his stamp on his films. The lavish style of life that the success of his motion pictures made possible was his enjoyment and his revenge on his poor youth and the survival games he played during his refugee years. He was the last film czar, but also the last of the great creative producers. As Fred Zinnemann says, "The other 'creative producers' are ridiculous. It is vanity."

The last time I saw Spiegel was three months before his death, dispensing champagne and generosity in his Park Avenue apartment. The redecoration was complete, he could revel among his paintings forever. For New York without Spiegel would seem like Manhattan without the Empire State Building. He was particularly proud of a Soutine hung on a wire. He pulled it aside to reveal a television screen, which could show on video all his major films. Behind the paintings was the man who made the pictures, and put his life into the making of them. His death left a void among thousands of people and a vacuum in the film industry that will not be filled.

Acknowledgments

I am most indebted to Michael Lindsay, who has interviewed so many leading people in the film industry for the benefit of this book, and my wife Sonia, who has encouraged me to seek the truth about Samuel Spiegel. I am also deeply grateful to all the people listed below who have contributed through interviews or writing to my understanding of this remarkable man. All the opinions and judgments, however, are my responsibility.

Polly Adler, Michael A. Anderegg, Franz Antel

Lauren Bacall, Tino Balio, Jerry Bauer, John Baxter, Peter Beale, Frawley Becker, Baroness Bentinck, Laurence Bergreen, Alain Bernheim, Lord Bernstein, Stephen Birmingham, Dirk Bogarde, Humphrey Bogart, Robert Bolt, Melvyn Bragg, Joseph Breen, Mr. and Mrs. Albert Broccoli, Peter Brook, Adrian Brunel, John Bryson, Peter Bull, Bridget Byrne

Jack Cardiff, Chris Chase, John Cheever, Eddie Chodorov, Michel Ciment, Bosley Crowther.

Tom Dardis, the Earl of Dudley, Philip Dunne

Anne Edwards, Amos Elon, Edward Z. Epstein, Laurence Evans, William K. Everson.

Douglas Fairbanks, Jnr., Stephen Farber, Rudi Fehr, Albert Finney, James F. Fixx, Guy Flatley, Charles Foley, Jane Fonda, Mrs. Christina Ford, Ivan Foxwell, Mike Frankovich, Philip French, Willy Frischauer

Zsa Zsa Gabor, Rita Gam, Nadia Gardiner, Kenneth L. Geist, Robert Emmett Ginna, Milton Goldman, Samuel Goldwyn, Ezra Goodman, Charles Gordon, Douglas Gosling, Morton Gottleib, Bill and Betty Graf, Fred Lawrence Guiles, Sir Alec Guinness.

Mrs. Jack Hawkins, Radie Harris, Sterling Hayden, Ben Hecht, Lillian Hellman, Katharine Hepburn, Charles Higham, Jack Hildyard, Patricia Hodge, William Holden, Mrs. Arthur Hornblow, John Houseman, John Huston, Joe Hyams.

Leo Jaffe, Marion Javits, Erskine Johnson, David Jones

Pauline Kael, Stuart Kaminsky, Elliott Kastner, Tessa Kennedy Kastner, Stanley Kauffman, Elia Kazan, Buster Keaton, Lady ("Slim") Keith, Mr. and Mrs. Thomas Kempner, Jennifer Kent, Evelyn Keyes, Paul Kohner, Teddy Kolleck, Bob Koster

Carl Laemmle, Hedy Lamarr, Burt Lancaster, Kenneth Lane, Fritz Lang, Abe

Lastfogel, Patricia Kennedy Lawford, Irving Lazar, James Leahy, Barbara Leaming, Sir David Lean, Albert Lewin, David Lewin, Mark Littman, Si Litvinoff, Mary Anita Loos, Yigal Lossin

Brenda Maddox, Axel Madsen, Christopher Manckiewicz, Roderick Mann, Stanley Mann, Johnny Maschio, Paul Mayersberg, Mercedes McCambridge, Golda Meir, Lady Melchett, Eileen Melmont, Ivan Moffatt, Pandora Mond, Caroline Moorehead, Joe Morella, Constantin Morros, Robert Muller, Michael Munn

Conrad Nagel, Victor S. Navasky, Nadia Nerina, Robert de Niro, Sir Anthony and Lady Nutting

Philip Oakes, Edna O'Brien, Lord Olivier, Peter O'Toole

Michael Pasternak, Mr. and Mrs. Samuel Peabody, Arthur Penn, Ann Pennington, Frank and Eleanor Perry, Diana Phipps, Gene D. Phillips, Harold and Lady Antonia Pinter, S. Lee Pogostin, Baron and Baroness Enrico di Portonova, Gerald Pratley, Werner Preusser

Jane Rayne, Mr. and Mrs. Rayner, Rex Reed, Gottfried and Sylvia Reinhardt, Lisl Reisch, Edward G. Robinson, Nicholas and Luke Roeg, Lady Rothermere, Janice Rule

Sidney Sapir, Ted Scaife, Arthur and Alexandra Schlesinger, Philip K. Scheuer, Budd Schulberg, Mrs. Milton Shulman, Nancy Lynn Schwartz, Irene Mayer Selznick, Omar Sharif, Marcus Sieff, Alan Silcocks, Elliot Silverstein, Frank Sinatra, Jean Kennedy Smith, Maud Spector, Adam Spiegel, Joanne Stang, Rod Steiger, David Sterritt, George Stevens, Geraldine Stultz

Elizabeth Taylor, John Russell Taylor, Bob Thomas, Keith Turner

Peter Ustinov

William van der Heuvel, Dennis van Thal, Jean Murray Vanderbilt, Bayard Veiller, Gore Vidal, Salka and Peter Viertel

Walter Wanger, Nicholas Wapshott, Baroness Stephanie von Watzdorf, Lord Weidenfeld, Bernard Weinraub, Orson Welles, Corinthia West, Michael White, Douglas Whitney, Billy Wilder, Tennessee Williams, William Wolf, Sir John Woolf, C. Wright Mills, Mrs. Williams ("Talli") Wyler

Terence Young, Max Youngstein

Mike Zimring, Fred Zinnemann, Adolph Zukor

Selected Bibliography

I am indebted to the following authors for their works, which have so much aided my own work:

Polly Adler. *A House Is Not a Home* (London, 1954).
Michael A. Anderegg. *David Lean* (Boston, 1984).

Isaac Babel. *Collected Stories* (New York, 1960).
Tino Balio. *United Artists: The Company Built by the Stars* (Madison, Wisc., 1976).
John Baxter. *The Hollywood Exiles* (London, 1976)
Laurence Bergreen. *James Agee: A Life* (New York, 1984).
Stephen Birmingham. *"Our Crowd": The Great Jewish Families of New York* (New York, 1967).
Adrian Brunel. *Nice Work: The Story of Thirty Years in British Film Production* (London, 1949).
Peter Bull. *Bulls in the Meadows* (London, 1959).
———. *I Say, Look Here!* (London, 1965).

John Caute. *The Fellow Travellers,* (London, 1973).
Michel Ciment. *Le Livre de Losey* (Paris, 1979).
———. *Kazan on Kazan* (London, 1973)
Lester Cole. *Hollywood Red: The Autobiography of Lester Cole* (Palo Alto, 1981).
Noël Coward. *Noël Coward Diaries* (Boston, 1982).
Bosley Crowther. *The Lion's Share: The Story of an Entertainment Empire* (New York, 1957).

Tom Dardis. *Keaton: The Man Who Wouldn't Lie Down* (London, 1979).
Norman Davies. *God's Playground: A History of Poland,* vol.II (Oxford, 1981).
Philip Dunne. *Take Two* (New York. 1980).
Olivier D'Etchegoyen. *The Comedy of Poland* (London, 1924).

Anne Edwards. *Katharine Hepburn* (London, 1985).
Amos Elon. *The Israelis: Fathers and Sons* (London, 1971).
William K. Everson. *American Silent Film* (Oxford, 1978).

Philip French. *The Movie Moguls* (London, 1969).
Willy Frischauer. *Behind the Scenes of Otto Preminger* (London, 1973).

Kenneth L. Geist. *Pictures Will Talk: The Life and Films of Joseph L. Mankiewicz* (New York, 1978).
Ezra Goodman. *The Fifty-Year Decline and Fall of Hollywood* (New York, 1961).

Fitzhugh Greene. *Film Finds Its Tongue* (New York, 1929).
Fred Lawrence Guiles. *Hanging On in Paradise* (New York, 1975).
Alec Guinness. *Blessings in Disguise* (London 1986).

Radie Harris. *Radie's World* (New York, 1975).
Jack Hawkins. *Anything for a Quiet Life* (London, 1973).
Sterling Hayden. *Wanderer* (New York, 1963).
Ben Hecht. *A Child of the Century* (New York, 1964).
Charles Higham. *Charles Laughton* (New York, 1976).
———. *Hollywood Cameramen: Sources of Light* (London, 1970).
———. *Orson Welles: The Rise and Fall of an American Genius* (New York, 1986).
Charles Higham and Joel Greenberg. *The Celluloid Muse: Hollywood Directors Speak* (London, 1969).
Foster Hirsch. *Joseph Losey* (Boston, 1980).
E. Nils Holstius. *Hollywood Through the Back Door* (London, 1937).
John Houseman. *Front and Center* (New York, 1979).
John Huston. *An Open Book* (London, 1981).
Joe Hyams. *Bogart and Bacall: A Love Story* (London, 1975).
———. *Bogie: The Biography of Humphrey Bogart* (New York, 1966).

"The Jewish Case." *Before the Anglo-American Committee of Inquiry on Palestine* (Jerusalem, 1947).

Pauline Kael: *When the Lights Go Down* (London, 1979).
———. *Kiss Kiss Bang Bang* (London, 1970).
Stuart Kaminsky. *John Huston: Maker of Magic* (Boston, 1978).
Stanley Kauffman. *Living Images* (New York, 1975).
Buster Keaton: *My Wonderful World of Slapstick* (London, 1967).
Evelyn Keyes. *Scarlett O'Hara's Younger Sister* (Secaucus, N.J., 1977).
Thomas Kiernan. *Jane Fonda: An Intimate Biography* (London, 1973).
Jon Kimche. *Palestine or Israel* (London, 1973).
Arthur Koestler. *Promise and Fulfilment, Palestine 1917–1949* (London, 1949).
Richard Koszarski. *Hollywood Directors, 1941–1976 (New York, 1977)*.

Hedy Lamarr. *Ecstasy and Me* (New York, 1966).
James Leahy. *The Cinema of Joseph Losey* (London, 1967).
Barbara Leaming. *Orson Welles* (London, 1985).
Yigal Lossin. *Pillar of Fire: The Rebirth of Israel/A Visual History* (Jerusalem, 1986).
Noah Lucas. *The Modern History of Israel* (London, 1975).

Joseph F. McCrindle. *Behind the Scenes* (London, 1971).

W. D. McCrackan. *The New Palestine* (London, 1922).

Brenda Maddox. *Who's Afraid of Elizabeth Taylor?* (New York, 1977).

Axel Madsen. *John Huston* (London, 1979).

———. *William Wyler* (New York, 1973).

———. *Billy Wilder* (London, 1968).

John Marlowe. *The Seat of Pilate* (London, 1959).

Paul Mayersberg. *Hollywood: The Haunted House* (London, 1967).

Golda Meir. *Speaks Out* (London, 1973).

Caroline Moorehead. *Sidney Bernstein* (London, 1984).

Joe Morella and Edward Z. Epstein. *Brando: The Unauthorized Biography* (London, 1973).

Michael Munn. *The Kid from the Bronx: A Biography of Tony Curtis* (London, 1984).

Victor S. Navasky. *Naming Names* (New York, 1980).

Roy Newquist. *Showcase* (New York, 1966).

Palestine. A Study of Arab and British Policies, vol I (New Haven, 1947).

Gene D. Phillips. *Artists in an Industry* (Chicago, 1973).

Gerald Pratley. *The Cinema of David Lean* (London, 1974).

———. *The Cinema of John Huston* (New York, 1977).

———. *The Cinema of Otto Preminger* (New York, 1971).

Edward G. Robinson (with Leonard Spiegelgass). *All my Yesterdays* (New York, 1973).

Bernard Rosenberg and Harry Silverstein. *The Real Tinsel* (London, 1970).

Lillian Ross. *Picture* (New York, 1953).

Leo C. Rosten. *Hollywood, The Movie Colony, The Movie Makers* (New York, 1941).

Joseph Roth. *Flight Without End* (London, 1977).

———.*The Silent Prophet* (London, 1980).

———.*The Emperor's Tomb* (London, 1984).

Adela Rogers St. Johns. *Love, Laughter & Tears* (New York, 1978).

Horace B. Samuel. *Unholy Memories of the Holy Land* (London, 1930).

Richard Schickel. *Common Fame: The Culture of Celebrity* (London, 1985).

Budd Schulberg. *On the Waterfront: A Screenplay with Afterword* (Carbondale, Ill., 1980).

Bruno Schulz. *Cinnamon Shops* (London, 1963).

———. *Sanitorium Under the Sign of the Hourglass* (London, 1979).

Nancy Lynn Schwartz. *The Hollywood Writers' Wars* (New York, 1982).

Steve Seidman. *The Film Career of Billy Wilder* (Boston, 1977).

Irene Mayer Selznick. *A Private View* (London, 1985).

Omar Sharif. *The Eternal Male* (London, 1977).

Eric Sherman and Martin Rubin. *The Director's Event* (New York, 1970).

Upton Sinclair Presents William Fox (Pasadena, 1933).

Alan Silver and James Ursini. *David Lean and his Films* (London, 1974).

Neil Sinyard and Adrian Turner. *Journey Down Sunset Boulevard: The Films of Billy Wilder* (Isle of Wight, 1979).

H. Allen Smith. *Low Man on a Totem Pole* (Philadelphia, 1941).

Anthony Summers. *Goddess: The Secret Lives of Marilyn Monroe* (London, 1985).

John Russell Taylor. *Strangers in Paradise: The Hollywood Emigrés 1933–1950* (London, 1983).

Bob Thomas. *King Cohn: The Life and Times of Harry Cohn* (New York, 1967).

————. *Golden Boy: The Untold Story of William Holden* (London, 1982).

Margaret Thorp. *America at the Movies.* (New Haven, 1937).

Peter Viertel. *White Hunter, Black Heart* (New York, 1953).

Salka Viertel. *The Kindness of Strangers* (New York, 1969).

Alexander Walker. *The Celluloid Sacrifice* (London, 1966).

Nicholas Wapshott. *Peter O'Toole* (London, 1983).

Herman G. Weinberg. *A Manhattan Odyssey* (New York, 1982).

Louis Wirth. *The Ghetto* (Chicago, 1928).

Tennessee Williams. *Memoirs* (London, 1976).

Norman Zierold. *The Hollywood Tycoons* (London, 1969).

Articles

I am much indebted to the following articles and references in magazines to Spiegel:

"Arthur Penn Objects," *New York Times* (20 February 1966).
Robert Bolt. "The Playwright in Films," *Saturday Review* (29 December 1962).
Peter Brook. "Lord of the Flies," *Sight and Sound* (Summer 1963).
Bridget Byrne. "Sam Spiegel: Making Cathedrals out of Raw Film," *Los Angeles Times* (2 January 1972).
Chris Chase. "At the Movies," *New York Times* (18 February 1983).
Cue Magazine (28 December 1957).

Victor Davis, "Hollywood's Old Lion Roars Again," London *Daily Express*, (5 June 1982).

Stephen Farber. "Hollywood Takes on 'The Last Tycoon,'" *New York Times*, (21 March 1976).
James F. Fixx. "The Spiegel Touch," *Saturday Review* (29 December 1962).
Guy Flatley. "Don't Ask Them to Go on Daddy Sam's Yacht," *New York Times* (12 April 1970).
Charles Foley. "The Stuff that Dreams Are Made Of," London *Observer*, (30 March 1976).

"Grand Illusions," Emerson College Film Society, Boston, Mass. (February 1977).

Radie Harris. *Hollywood Reporter* (13 January 1986).
"Hollywood: The Emperor," *Time* (19 April 1963).
John Huston. *Theatre Arts* (June 1952).

Erskine Johnson. "What Makes Sammy Sail?" *Los Angeles Mirror*, (9 June 1961).
Harlan Jacobson. "Big Tusker," *Film Comment* (April 1983).

Elia Kazan. *Movie*, No. 19 (Winter 1971–72).
Kine Weekly. (19 March and 9 April 1936).

David Lewin. "Sam, the Movie Maker," London *Daily Mail* (8 March 1971).
Yigal Lossin. "Pillar of Fire, 1914–1929," Channel 4 TV (21 October 1986).

Norman Mailer. "Superman Comes to the Supermarket," *Esquire* (October 1960).
Roderick Mann. "Too Much Money Is Making Actors Unhappy, Says Spiegel," *Sunday Express* (27 June 1982).
Robert Muller. "The Last Tycoon," London *Daily Mail* (20 April 1959).

New York (21 January 1980).

Newsweek (28 December 1959)

Philip Oakes. "Sam Spiegel," London *Sunday Times* (14 November 1971).

T. M. Pryor. "Long Time No See Hollywood," *Variety* (23 January 1963).

"Questioning Miss Hellman on Movies," *New York Times* (28 February 1966).

Rex Reed, "Penn: And Where Did All The Chase-ing Lead?" *New York Times* (13 February 1966).

———— "Rex Reed Replies," *New York Times* (20 February 1966).

Sidney Sapir *Screen International* (1 January 1986).

Philip K. Scheuer. "Movie Industry Could Sell the World on America," *Los Angeles Times Calendar* (4 November 1965).

Budd Schulberg. "'Waterfront': From Docks to Film," *New York Times* (11 July 1954).

———— "Why Write It when You Can't Sell It to the Pictures?" *Saturday Review* (3 September 1955).

"Sessue Hayakawa," *Films and Filming*, (February 1962).

Joanne Stang. "Lancaster Swims to Deeper Waters," *New York Times* (14 August 1966).

"A Statement from Sam Spiegel," *The Spectator* (6 May 1960).

David Sterritt. "Spiegel," *Christian Science Monitor* (17 March 1983).

C. Hooper Trash. "German Screen Notes," *New York Times* (18 February 1932).

Universal Filmlexicon (1932).

Bernard Weinraub. "Director Arthur Penn Takes on General Custer," *New York Times* (21 December 1969).

William Wolf. "Doing It His Way," *New York* (21 February 1983).

Newspaper References

I am also much indebted to the following newspaper references to Spiegel.

New York Times	18 February 1932
	15 April 1951
	2 March 1952
	11 July 1953
	23 May 1954
	19 May 1957
	23 March 1958
	5 June 1958
	26 March 1961
	15 July 1962
	3 and 26 January 1963
	17 August 1964
	20 June 1965
	15 December 1968
	21 December 1969
	12 April 1970
	24 November 1973
	18 February 1983
Los Angeles Citizen	8 December 1943
Los Angeles Citizen-News	9 April 1958
Los Angeles Daily News	13 September 1947
	5 December 1947
Los Angeles Examiner	6 January 1954
	2 December 1957
Los Angeles Herald-Examiner	23 April 1980
Los Angeles Mirror	9 June 1961
Los Angeles Mirror-News	8 January 1958
Los Angeles Times	8 December 1943
	8 October 1952
	24 November 1953
	20 June 1982
	1 January 1986
Variety	3 February 1965
London *Sunday Times*	29 March 1987

INDEX